PRAISE FOR *F THE FUNNEL*

"Revenue generation is the heart and soul of a repeatable and predictable marketing function within any organization. Jeff clearly outlines the path to a new point of view for your sales and marketing teams. It's all about relationships. With the expanded role marketing enjoys—or should enjoy—with any smart company, forging a strong relationship with customer success, sales, engineering, and other departments will lead to success. Revenue success."

—*Jeanne Hopkins, chief revenue officer, HappyNest*

"As a leader in marketing and customer engagement for the past fifteen years, I have always sought to take the best approaches to develop repeatable, predictable, and scalable revenue. As a repeat CMO, I have experienced what it takes to earn a seat and a voice at the revenue table. Jeff's book delivers. I have used many of these concepts over the years to build my global marketing teams. Implement the Loop today!"

—*Meagen Eisenberg, chief revenue officer, TripActions*

"*F the Funnel* transforms your thinking to be more proactive, customer centric, and strategic and will elevate marketing's value to the business."

—*Jim Kruger, chief marketing officer, Veeam Software*

"A witty and informed view of the rough lot in life we marketers choose when we perpetuate the behaviors that got us here. This is about rethinking everything about the hamster wheel of creating demand. It is about getting on a more sustainable path of customer engagement and having a lot of fun getting to 'ring the bell' of revenue."

—*Stephanie Meyer, head of marketing, Webster Bank*

"I know that what Jeff is writing about is real. A particularly marketing-savvy and genuinely future-focused board member reached out at one of my prior companies to ask what my preferred future path would be, because the accountability for the success or failure of a company is stacked against the CMO. The executive committee votes on a strategy together and when it doesn't work, the CMO is the one blamed as if everyone else wasn't there. These continual transitions make it hard for any marketing department to get traction in a world where customers are more discerning and less tolerant. The funnel is long overdue for a rewrite. Help us make it happen, Jeff!"

—*Maggie Lower, chief marketing officer, Cision*

"As the marketing leader who brought inflight internet to the US markets in 2008 and has delivered billions in incremental top-line revenue across the telecom, pharma, financial services, and education industries, I can say unequivocally that the funnel is dead. If you are stuck and haven't transformed, the time is now. We partnered with the team at TPG, and back in December 2015 we launched our new capabilities. This accelerated our marketing paradigm shift with how we aligned our sales and marketing teams and how we developed flexible anchor solutions (systems)—all with a laser focus on unlocking the data along the customer journey so we can deepen those relationships and improve performance and customer outcomes. This stepping stone has led to our marketing team being the growth engine in the company while simultaneously being the group that led a broader cultural transformation across the company, which has helped us to be more innovative and, most recently, to be considered by leading experts as one of the most mature data-driven companies within education."

—*Jeff Tognola, SVP of commercial operations and chief marketing officer, Laureate Online Education & Walden University*

"Kudos to Jeff! He reminds us that our mission, as marketers, is to connect companies to customers. He challenges us to think beyond transactions and build relationships—deliver value and, in so doing, deliver revenue. Admittedly generations of 'successful' marketers have been raised on the funnel and waterfall models. But mix in educated buyers and unprecedented choice with the expectation of continuous client success, and the limitations of the funnel are clear. A few pages in, you'll recognize the reality of your typical day (maybe you'll chuckle or grimace), and by the closing chapter, you'll have the blueprint for change—what's needed and how to go about it. Long live the Loop!"

—*Meg Murphy, chief marketing officer, IBM Systems, Quantum & Partner Ecosystem*

"Today, successful CMOs have high pain thresholds, but willpower is not a long-term strategy for growth. *F the Funnel* delivers both practical advice and inspirational strategies for changing this dynamic. Instead of seeking loyal customers, marketers need to pivot and serve as loyal brands."

—*Jamie Gutfreund, global chief marketing officer, MGA Entertainment*

"Jeff was kind enough to give me a preview of the book, and he definitely grabbed my attention right from the start. I've been in the marketing field for quite a while now, and I've worked closely with sales my whole career. I can tell you with 100 percent certainty that Jeff deeply understands the complex, uneasy, and often challenging relationship between marketing and sales in the enterprise. As we know, understanding the problem is half the solution. This gives me high confidence that Jeff's book will go a long way to improve how effectively you work with your counterparts."

—*Nick Panayi, chief marketing officer, Amelia*

"*F the Funnel* hits the nail right on the head. It speaks in depth, from extensive experience, about the challenges today's marketers face and the change that is necessary to evolve the perception of marketing as a cost center to a revenue-generating asset. Jeff provides great insight into the mind shift marketers must undergo to ensure the process does not stop at the sale but continues on into developing a relationship with your customers, ensuring customer success, and creating advocates. Truly a great read for any marketer or leader looking to take their marketing department, and organization, to the next level.

—*Erica Hay Thompson, chief marketing officer, Human Health Project*

"Jeff has long been a force in marketing data and science and has compiled some of his best nuggets of advice and wisdom in *F The Funnel*. Chock-full of examples, war stories, and simple truths all wrapped in a better way forward, this book is a must-read."

—*Julie Roehm, chief marketing and experience officer, Party City Holdings Inc.*

With his signature straightforward and engaging narrative Jeff explains how the Loop builds customer loyalty and advocacy. Keep it handy; you will keep going back to this book while you work your way into adopting the Loop."

—*Sergio Corbo, chief commercial officer, Veolia*

"Inspired reading for experienced C-suite marketers and newcomers to the CMO role alike, *F the Funnel* charts a clear path for reinventing revenue generation. Jeff's style is engaging and informed, and his advice is actionable and relevant."

—*Amy Barzdukas, chief marketing officer, Omnitracs*

"In the ongoing battle for marketing to solidify its role as a revenue center versus a cost center, no other construct has done as much to undermine success as the 'lead funnel.' With his view of the funnel as 'a liability, driving wedges between us, our customers, and our potential revenue,' Pedowitz pulls no punches in debunking the funnel. His new approach proposes to accelerate growth while building longer, more rewarding relationships with customers. Bring it!"

—*Wendy White, chief marketing officer, TigerConnect*

"A practical and informed view of marketing demand generation, its promise and its pitfalls, and how relationships are at the heart of sustainable growth. With the strategic role marketing enjoys—or should enjoy—with any smart company, forging strong relationships with customer success, sales, engineering, and other departments will lead to success. Revenue success."

—*Marianna Kantor, chief marketing officer, Esri*

"Building customer relationships and growing revenue through marketing requires a dramatic shift in our approach, ultimately discarding the funnel and looking at ongoing nonstop engagement with our customers to learn, innovate, and grow. The Loop provides a practical guide for the next evolution of marketing."

—*Marie Hattar, chief marketing officer, Keysight Technologies*

"*F the Funnel* is a must-read for marketers and other go-to-market leaders who want to build healthy businesses and avoid the pitfalls so many companies face today."

—*David Cain, chief marketing officer, Lattice*

"This is a must-read primer for all marketers and marketing enthusiasts. The anecdotes and facts have aptly presented the plight of a marketer in a very lucid manner. More than that, Jeff showed the other side of the tunnel, or rather funnel, which is not only exciting but also enlightening."

—*Sukirti Panigrahi, associate director, Deloitte*

"Brilliantly written and relevant in today's landscape of digital disruption, Jeff Pedowitz disposes of old ideologies and the overused 'standard ROI funnel' in place of a modernized customer-centric marketing solution that effectively embraces their customer's needs and desires through a journey of transformation to becoming clients for life. A must-read for every CEO, CMO, and marketing strategist looking to remain relevant."

—*Paul Lucido, chief marketing officer, PRMG*

"Jeff's call to arms for marketers to focus on customer experience to drive revenue and away from managing the funnel is spot on. Loyalty and advocacy are critical drivers of long-term sustainable revenue and are won by those who focus on customers rather than a static, one-size-fits-all model. Dynamic, ongoing, real-time interaction and customer insights are gold—and those that capture and act fast will deliver superior brand experiences, repeat customers, and revenue. Take heed!"

—*Sophie Chesters, senior vice president and chief marketing officer, Medallia*

"A must-read for business leaders who need a pragmatic and, I must say, a modern approach to leveraging marketing properly. No longer should we be thinking of a linear demand-generation funnel. Marketing has a more significant role to play for driving revenue— from the first to every interaction with a customer—but you need a path forward. This book shows us that path. I have known Jeff for years, and he brings a wealth of experience and a frankness that is refreshing and, more importantly, valuable. Enjoy the read!"

—*Drew Clarke, chief strategy officer, Qlik*

"The emphasis and examination of go-to-market alignment and results have never been greater. Jeff's transitional thinking from a sales- and marketing-generated funnel to the notion of a 'Loop' aligns the impact of marketing in a more holistic manner. In a services- and subscription-driven world, Jeff's approach can drive more cohesive and predictable results, and that is good news for any organization."

—*Wes Durow, chief marketing officer, Extreme Networks*

"This isn't just a book for CMOs and senior marketers; it should be read by the whole C-suite. Jeff expertly defines why thinking about sales and marketing 'as a funnel' reduces customers to transactions. This ultimately impacts the most important thing a business has: it's relationships with customers."

—*Richard Jones, chief marketing officer, Cheetah Digital*

"As Jeff says in his book, marketing is hard during the best of times. And I think we can all agree that 2020 brought with it some of the worst of times. For marketers, not only did we need to contend with the rapid disappearance of physical events and the resulting oversaturation of digital channels, but we also had to fight for market share during extreme economic uncertainties. Not only were marketing budgets slashed and resources cut, but many marketing teams were being asked to make miracles happen.

Jeff's book, *F the Funnel*, is incredibly timely and tackles the real-world pressures marketing teams face today and provides a new and agile framework for marketers to follow. Bottom line, the world has changed, and the way people buy has changed—so why do marketers still rely on antiquated and linear methodologies of customer engagement and tracking marketing contribution? I highly recommend this book to any marketer who is looking to uplevel their game, develop dynamic relationships with customers, and raise the perception of marketing across their organization."

—*Dayna Rothman, chief marketing officer, OneLogin*

F THE FUNNEL

F THE FUNNEL

A NEW WAY TO ENGAGE
CUSTOMERS & GROW REVENUE

JEFF PEDOWITZ

ForbesBooks

Published by ForbesBooks, Charleston, South Carolina.
Member of Advantage Media Group.

ForbesBooks is a registered trademark, and the ForbesBooks colophon is a trademark of Forbes Media, LLC.

Printed in the United States of America.

10 9 8 7 6 5 4 3 2 1

ISBN: 978-1-95086-367-9
LCCN: 2021905008

This custom publication is intended to provide accurate information and the opinions of the author in regard to the subject matter covered. It is sold with the understanding that the publisher, Advantage|ForbesBooks, is not engaged in rendering legal, financial, or professional services of any kind. If legal advice or other expert assistance is required, the reader is advised to seek the services of a competent professional.

Advantage Media Group is proud to be a part of the Tree Neutral® program. Tree Neutral offsets the number of trees consumed in the production and printing of this book by taking proactive steps such as planting trees in direct proportion to the number of trees used to print books. To learn more about Tree Neutral, please visit **www.treeneutral.com**.

Since 1917, Forbes has remained steadfast in its mission to serve as the defining voice of entrepreneurial capitalism. ForbesBooks, launched in 2016 through a partnership with Advantage Media Group, furthers that aim by helping business and thought leaders bring their stories, passion, and knowledge to the forefront in custom books. Opinions expressed by ForbesBooks authors are their own. To be considered for publication, please visit **www.forbesbooks.com**.

To my wife, Cherie. Thank you for loving me and encouraging me every day to chase my dreams. Partners in life, partners in business. Best friends and soulmates. You are my everything. To my children—Alex, Zach, and Ashley—you inspire me every day. I love your creativity, your character, and your individuality.

CONTENTS

IT'S YOURS NOW

THE LOOP IS NOT AN ISLAND

INTRODUCTION

Every week I talk to dozens of marketing executives, and I hear a recurring theme: They work their rears off. They bring their A game. They add to the bottom line. But they're not feeling the love. They're being pressured, marginalized, elbowed out of their companies' game plans. This isn't what they signed up for.

Marketing departments are the creative souls of organizations. We who excel at marketing are able to combine psychology, art, technology, and statistics in cutting-edge ways that draw attention to our companies. We have the skills to connect customers to life-changing products and services. We tell the stories and create the artwork that bridge the gap between our companies and the outside world.

And we do all of this without ever losing sight of our KPIs and our companies' strategic focus. Without us, our companies wouldn't be able to sell a thing. Without us, they'd crash and burn.

And yet it often seems our companies don't respect us. While most marketing departments are brimming with great ideas, they don't have the institutional authority or credibility they need to secure resources like budgeting and staffing so they can execute on those ideas.

1

And that's in the *best* of times.

In the worst of times—when there's an economic slowdown or the company's stock takes a hit—things get even harder for us. CFOs rush to cut expenses. The first thing they cut is usually the travel budget; the second is, you know it, the marketing budget. After all, they can't cut R&D—the next generation of products needs to be engineered. They can't cut manufacturing or service—that's where all the revenue comes from. They can't cut sales because the sales team has the ability to run out the door and start generating revenue *now*.

So marketing's resources get slashed, again and again. And without those resources, our capacity to deliver—to follow through on a bold campaign or launch a new initiative—is drastically reduced. In short, we're set up for failure. And then, when we do fail, *we're* blamed. "See, I told you marketing wasn't giving us any ROI." Our authority and credibility plummet even further in a vicious cycle.

The result? Frustration. Disillusionment. Turnover. CMOs have some of the highest turnover rates among C-level executives, and our teams don't have much more job security than we do.

What's the Problem?

The heart of this issue is this: our companies see us as *cost* centers, not *revenue* centers. We're viewed as the make-it-pretty people, not as what we really are (or could be): the people who turn products and services into money by connecting companies to customers.

We need to change that perception, and to some extent, we need to change that reality too. We need to establish our departments as vital sources of revenue for our companies. Only then will we get the respect—and more importantly, the resources—we need and deserve.

A huge part of the problem is the model we've been using. For the past century-plus, the model sales and marketing teams have used for generating customer revenue has been the Funnel—or some version thereof.

The problem is, the Funnel is more of a sales construct than a marketing construct. And it doesn't even work very well for sales anymore, frankly. The Funnel was designed for a bygone era, one of traveling salesmen and matchbook advertising.

You know the Funnel. You've seen it a zillion times. Countless iterations of it have been put forth, but they all describe the same essential process of customer acquisition. You start by creating *awareness* (the customer becomes aware of your product), you then move your potential customers to *interest*, then *decision-making*, and finally to *action* (the customer converts to a sale). The widest group exists at the top of the Funnel. Then, as you work your marketing and sales magic, you narrow your prospects down to a smaller and smaller group that is more and more serious about buying your product. Until you reach the bottom. The sale.

And then what?

Nothing. The Funnel ends there.

But what about following up with customers so we can learn about *their* experience using our products and help them gain more value from our products? What about using the relationship we've built with customers to generate interest in some of our other product lines? What about turning satisfied customers into raving fans who will sell our products *for* us?

The Funnel doesn't care. The Funnel is a transactional model that is literally built to end. The Funnel is all about *our* experience, not the

> **The Funnel was designed for a bygone era, one of traveling salesmen and matchbook advertising.**

customer's. We get what we want from our customers—namely, the sale—and then we ditch them. One and done.

The Funnel is a bad model. At best, it's an incomplete one. In order to transform marketing departments into thriving revenue centers, we need to adopt a new model, one that is based on creating a *dynamic, ongoing* relationship with our customers—a relationship that, in many ways, doesn't end with the sale but *begins* with it.

That model exists. We call it the Loop. And that's what this book is about.

Why Listen to Me?

For over twenty years, I've been helping marketing departments reclaim authority, credibility, and, yes, job security by transforming themselves from cost centers into revenue centers. My company, the Pedowitz Group, has developed an unparalleled reputation in the marketing community by providing insight to clients on topics such as digital transformation, customer-centricity, business accountability, and marketing technology.

The Pedowitz Group is all about the revenue. My business partner and good friend, Dr. Debbie Qaqish, coined the phrase "revenue marketing," and for twelve-plus years, we have asked our clients to measure us not by what we *promise* them but by what we *deliver* to them: outcomes, pipeline, and engagement—all of which led to repeatable, predictable, and scalable revenue.

With over seventy expert consultants in twenty-four states, we have serviced over 1,500 corporate clients, many of which are household names from the Fortune 500—General Electric, Microsoft, Cisco Systems, Intel, New York Life, American Express, Morgan Stanley; the list goes on and on. We have launched over ten thousand marketing campaigns and helped generate over $25 billion in marketing-sourced and marketing-influenced revenue. Our clients have won over fifty industry awards.

I don't say any of this to self-advertise but to assure you that my company and I know marketing from every angle and approach. We know the challenges you face because we deal with those challenges every day. And we have developed solutions that really work—i.e., generate revenue. And now, for the first time, I am putting my company's playbook into print. I'm going to share with you what we share with our treasured clients: our proven strategy for winning back the authority you need in order to survive and thrive.

In this book, I'll examine how Funnels became the industry standard and how they've led us astray. I'll diagnose the noxious effect these models have had on our relationships with customers and demonstrate how Funnels are responsible for the decay of credibility and authority in our marketing departments.

Most importantly, I'll introduce you to a new method we've developed for marketing teams: the Loop. Using the Loop *will* put you on a path to bigger earnings and better relationships—with your customers, with your companies, and with your peers.

The Plan

Here's how I will present the ideas so they'll make the most practical sense to you. *F the Funnel* unfolds in four parts:

- In part I, we'll look at the daunting challenges marketing departments face and discover that many of these challenges derive from the sales model we've all trusted for so long: the Funnel. We'll see how this near-universal "customer-engagement model" has become a liability, driving wedges between us, our customers, and our potential revenue.

- In part II, we'll discover the Loop—a new model that more fully reflects the experiences and desires of both customers and companies. We'll see that while Funnels contort us into shortsighted postures, the Loop can help us build longer, more rewarding relationships with our customers.

- In part III, we'll learn more about how the Loop can be adapted and operationalized to suit the needs and workflows of individual companies.

- And finally, in part IV, we'll learn what it takes to build inter-departmental coalitions around our Loops, winning back the authority and credibility we so badly need.

At TPG, we teach the Loop to our clients every day, and we know it works. We've seen it transform organizations, and we are confident it will work for you. But make no mistake. The Loop will disrupt your company. Innovation disrupts—and that's a good thing. Implementing the Loop is a marathon, not a sprint. It will require hard work, committed leadership, and a solid change-management plan. The journey at times will be challenging, but the payoff is huge. Marketing *will* become a revenue driver. You *will* have a seat in the boardroom. Your customers *will* be raving fans. I invite you to take the journey with me. Let's dive in.

PART I

F THE FUNNEL

CHAPTER 1

WHY DON'T THEY LOVE US?

T he calls pour into our offices every week.

The CMO of a large financial services firm in San Francisco who works with multiple product lines can't get attribution for her marketing efforts and feels her team is being marginalized. She needs better visibility into sales performance, better reporting, and better insight so she can show what her team is doing from a performance perspective.

A marketing executive in New York who works for a tight-budgeted start-up software company is under tremendous pressure to generate leads for the sales team and contribute to the pipeline. He needs help.

A CMO for a midsized company in Atlanta that deals with a relatively small niche market is trying to open up new buying centers and conversational groups within her existing accounts—but there are no mechanisms in place for her to engage at an account level because the model they're using is strictly transactional.

Marketing departments are being pressured, as never before, to prove their worth by delivering concrete, measurable results. And many of them *are* delivering great results. But they're struggling to demonstrate it. CMOs are eager to develop concrete mechanisms that will help them not only gain attribution for their present revenue contributions but also create exciting new sources of revenue they can own and execute. They're hungry to gain the same credibility as the VP of sales.

Why Does Sales Get the Love and We Don't?

"Jeff," said one near-desperate CMO in a recent call, "I really need your help."

"Sure," I said to him. "What can we do for you?"

"Well, my CEO pulled me and the VP of sales into his office last week and said the company wants us to increase sales by 20 percent in the next six months, and then he asked us both what we were going to do about it."

"Not an unheard-of challenge. So what did you tell him?"

"I talked about the strategy the marketing team was planning to use. I showed him all the campaigns we were going to launch and the channels we were going to leverage. I gave him a sample of the creatives we were going to throw at the problem. I showed him the plan I had come up with for getting everyone excited about the company's goal. On the dazzle meter, I was hitting about a nine-point-five out of ten."

I laughed. "Sounds good so far."

"Yeah, until the CEO turns to the VP of sales and says, 'What are *you* going to do to get sales up by 20 percent?' And the VP of sales says, 'That's easy. Give me marketing's budget. I'll go hire twenty salespeople, put them in our twenty best markets. Ten of them will hit their number. Bam, we'll be up 20 percent. And I'll do it by Christmas.'"

"So what happened?"

"The CEO gave all my money to the VP of sales, not me."

This scenario repeats itself over and over again in businesses across the globe. Why? Because it's a tried-and-true formula. In most cases, if you hire enough salespeople, you can get your numbers up. Companies know that half the sales team won't make quota, but they don't care. Hiring salespeople is just a cost of doing business. When more customers are needed, you just go out and hire more sales reps. You can measure the results, and you have historical data: Here's how many reps we hired. This was their quota. This is how many deals they brought in.

It's all very predictable from a math standpoint. In the case of marketing, however, things are usually not so predictable.

MARKETING AND REVENUE

It wasn't long ago that marketing didn't need to worry about revenue at all. Throughout most of the twentieth century, marketing departments were not responsible in any way, shape, or form for even generating *leads*, let alone actual revenue. All they had to do was create brand, advertise, run events, and launch products. They were the arts and crafts department.

It was only in the first decade of the 2000s, when systems such as Salesforce and marketing platforms entered the fray, that marketing first became accountable for generating leads and then, shortly afterward, for generating pipeline and revenue. Search engines, online advertising, social marketing—these weren't even concepts in the early 1990s. So, in the grand history of modern marketing, which goes back to the late 1800s, it's really only been in the last fifteen years or so that marketing has had to be responsible for revenue.

Sales, on the other hand, has been responsible for revenue since the beginning of time. Sales departments know all about the numbers. Numbers are their lifeblood. They know if they don't hit their target number by their target date, they're gone. And they're fine with that. That's the game they signed up for. Their respect and credibility have always flowed from numbers.

MARKETING IS ART ... *AND* SCIENCE

Marketing has been slow to realize that, like it or not, credibility comes from hard numbers—data, metrics, dollars. This is not an easy pill to swallow for people who come from the "art" side of the fence. Yes, marketers need to be awesome at telling the story, at developing an emotional connection with their brands, so they can connect their companies to their customers; that is a vitally important part of a marketer's job. But marketing also has to drive the numbers—the "science" side. Marketing must be both art and science.

The reason many marketers struggle so much is they have a hard time with the science. That doesn't mean they're stupid or bad at math. Far from it. Most marketers I know are highly intelligent and expansive thinkers. It just means they have trouble articulating, measuring, analyzing, and getting attribution for the things they're doing.

Alas, the CFO doesn't have that problem. Ultimately, the CFO looks at a single number when it comes to marketing: return on investment. ROI. "I gave you x dollars last year. How much new net revenue did we gain from those dollars? And how did you do compared to last year?" If your ROI is flat or down from last year, then in the CFO's mind, you're not being a good steward of your dollars. So you're probably going to get less money for the upcoming year. Simple formula. And many marketing executives don't seem to understand that basic math.

TIMELINES AND PRESSURE POINTS

On the other hand, marketing teams are often put in an unfair position. They're tasked to work at a long-term, big-picture level but are often "penalized" for failing to deliver short-term results.

Marketing tends to operate on longer timelines than sales, which is accustomed to being under pressure to perform every day, every month, every quarter. Marketing's work is more strategic. Marketing campaigns often unfold in stages over months and even years. For marketing teams, revenue generation takes place over longer time frames and in less measurable ways.

Also, marketing teams wear a lot of hats that are not strictly related to revenue. They have many "customers" besides the actual customers who buy the products. They must serve and satisfy the sales department, IT, partners, vendors, analysts, and so on. They are often asked to run various kinds of campaigns that are not about driving revenue but about building brand. They manage product marketing and marketing communications, they run events, they may work on innovation initiatives or manage the customer experience.

But here is where the "unfairness" comes in. While most company leaders do care about long-term strategy, they tend to keep a sharper eye on the *right now*. That's because they have stakeholders to answer to. If they're a public company, they have quarterlies for which they're held accountable. If they're in a private company, they have a board to report to. So their attitude is often "Hey, Marketing, I can't wait a year for you to work on your long-term BS that *might* someday produce results. What can you do for me now?"

That same nervous CEO, on the other hand, can easily pick up the phone and say, "Hey, Sales, can you go out and hustle me up a couple of deals?" The sales team then hurries out and brings in a couple of deals that help the company make its numbers for the quarter. And the CEO says, "Great job, Sales. You guys are going to Hawaii!"

Sales gets the plaques, the rewards, and the credibility because they produce the all-important short-term results. Meanwhile, marketing is left saying, "But I thought we agreed that our campaign was going to be a two-year plan and that we would all be patient."

And as I said earlier, things only get worse for marketing when economics take a downturn. If the board thinks for a minute that they're going to have a slow quarter or if a year gets off to a bad start, they're likely going to cut the budget, and marketing is going to be the first department sliced. Or if something unexpected happens—a new regulation drops or a competitor makes a surprise move—and the stock price takes a hit, the board's going to make substantial cuts to show the analysts that the company's running lean and mean. Marketing gets whacked again until the stock price comes back up.

That hundred grand you were promised for your initiative is now either gone or trimmed to a pittance. In turn, the ill-funded initiative fails in a sort of self-fulfilling prophecy.

So marketing, which traditionally operates under longer time frames, often ends up subjected to the same short-term pressure points as sales teams. But sales departments are designed to respond to such pressure points and timelines; marketing departments usually aren't.

A TOLL TAKEN

Turnover is the result of all this. When the marketing executive's unsupported initiative falls predictably flat, the executive may quit out of frustration or may get fired. Or, in other cases, the CMO's path out the door is one of gradual disillusionment or burnout.

After all, we marketing people tend to be idealists. We want to believe we can make a difference. Our job is not just about the money to us; we want to create something exciting and see it through to fruition. And we get frustrated when our efforts are systematically squelched.

When we interviewed for the job and got hired, that was like the wedding and the honeymoon.

But then we find ourselves in the reality of the marriage. Those amazing "master plans" we drew up on the whiteboard at home have been back-burnered indefinitely, and now we're just putting out fires, playing politics, covering our butts. Our partners are yelling at us, sales is pounding on our door making demands. Our teams are complaining because they don't have the tools they were promised (because the budget was cut). All that great support the CEO promised us has evaporated in the crisis-of-the-day environment.

Divorce is imminent.

A marketing executive's journey from wedded bliss to divorce is a short one compared to other C-level executives. Most CMOs are in their jobs only forty-three months, while their counterparts (CIO, 4.1 years; CHRO, 5 years; CFO, 5.1 years; and CEO, 8 years) tend to enjoy longer tenure.

But here's the message I want you to take from this book: the vast majority of the pressures that contribute to high turnover in marketing departments come down to one simple fact:

Our companies don't love us.

Why don't they love us? Because they see us as a *cost* center, not a *revenue* center. They don't really believe we contribute to the bottom line.

They may understand on an abstract level that our work helps sell products, but they don't see us as an essential cog in the revenue-generating machinery. Thus, no love.

It's All About Relationships

Relationships are at the heart of the matter. Most of the frustrated CMOs I talk to every week describe strained relationships with their companies and with their peers in other departments. In order to change our company's perception of us, we need to change our relationship with the company.

In order to change our company's perception of us, we need to change our relationship with the company.

And the way we do that—in broad strokes—is via a four-step cycle.

Let's look at the four stages of this cycle by viewing them as quadrants on a graph:

1. Poor Company Relationship
- Marketing is a cost concern
- No authority or credibility
- Reduced resources
- Missed targets
- Higher turnover

4. Good Company Relationship
- Marketing is a revenue center
- Authority, credibility, change agent
- Increased resources
- Repeatable, predictable, scalable
- Career security

2. Poor Customer Relationship
- Leads and activities
- Transactional
- Funnel based
- Missed targets
- Narcissism

3. Good Customer Relationship
- Customer experience
- Relationship oriented
- Loop based
- Achieved targets
- Customer clarity

Bad Relationships

Good Relationships

1. POOR COMPANY RELATIONSHIP

Here's where we are right now. Many of us presently have a poor relationship with our company. As long as the company views marketing as a cost center instead of a revenue center, our relationship with the company will continue to be fraught. It will be marked by disrespect and reactivity based on our inability to demonstrate the vital contributions we're making to the business. And we will continue to lack authority or credibility.

This poor relationship reduces our access to resources like budgeting and staffing, which then sets up the marketing department for future failures, ensuring a vicious cycle of ever-dwindling returns.

If we wish to improve our relationship with our company, there are a couple of things we can do. We might try bringing in a consultant to help us calculate our ROI so we can prove our value to the company. That can help. But really what we need is a more robust, long-term solution. And ultimately there's only one such solution available to us: we can start bringing in more revenue.

To do that, we need to forge stronger relationships with the people who *provide* revenue: our customers.

2. POOR CUSTOMER RELATIONSHIP

This is the stage where we discover that we aren't bringing in revenue because we aren't really connected to our customers. And that's not their fault, it's ours.

The main reason we're disconnected from our customers is that we're approaching our customers through Funnels—transactional models designed to reflect *our* desires and experiences, not theirs. That is, lure the customer, make the sale, done.

Using the Funnel forces us into bad behaviors with the customer. It impels us to think of them as a transaction, an entity we need to move from the top of the Funnel to the bottom of the Funnel ASAP. All we care about is getting the customer to the bell. We're not really focused on actually helping them. We get what we want from them, then we ditch them.

That's not a relationship, that's narcissism. Frankly, it's borderline sociopathy.

Only by understanding why we're failing can we start building better relationships with our customers …

3. GOOD CUSTOMER RELATIONSHIP

Here is where we turn things around. We come to realize that our relationship with the customer doesn't stop with getting them to the bell; rather, it keeps going in a cycle of continuous service.

This is where we abandon the Funnel and switch to the Loop (which we'll be explaining in detail as the book unfolds). We start focusing on the customer and building better relationships.

And when we start building healthier relationships with customers—surprise, surprise—they respond. Their lifetime value goes up. They buy more from us. We're now driving more revenue.

4. GOOD COMPANY RELATIONSHIP

In the fourth stage, the value of our improved customer relationships has its ultimate payoff. Now that we're bringing in revenue, we carry a new air of credibility. We can finally enjoy a closer, more rewarding relationship with our company and our peers—a relationship that's characterized by success, collaboration, job security, and mutual respect.

At last, we're invited into the boardroom. We have a seat at the table and a claim to some of the resources we were denied in the past.

To summarize this journey in four "acts":

1. Our relationship with our company is poor because our relationship with our customers is poor.

2. We realize that the Funnel model is the problem.

3. We throw out the Funnel and build a new model—the Loop—which helps us form better customer relationships. This leads to more revenue.

4. Our revenue production transforms our relationship with the company into a more fruitful one.

A Journey to Customer-Centricity

Throughout this book, we'll be talking about abandoning the Funnel for the Loop. But ultimately, what we'll *really* be talking about is transforming our vision about the work we do. There *is* a better way to engage our customers and build revenue. And that is by becoming truly customer centric.

I hear a lot of businesspeople talk about customer-centricity. But the question I ask them is: What are you doing about it? If you say you care about your customers but do nothing on a structural level to actually engage them, your care is only an abstraction—like people who say they care about the environment but don't recycle.

I'm not talking about mere customer *service*. There's a big difference between being customer-service oriented and being customer centric. A lot of us do care about our customers but only in a reactive way. The customer calls us with a problem, and we help them. The customer may feel they got good service because we were polite and resolved their issue. But did we learn whether they plan to buy again or whether they're getting value from what they bought from us? Do we know if they have other needs we might be able to help with?

Customer service is reactive. Customer-centricity is proactive. It involves actively finding out what the customer wants, when they want it, how they like to receive it, and what else they might need to make their experience complete—and giving it to them. The only way you know such things is by developing real, ongoing relationships with the customer.

And so this book is about not only redesigning your Funnel to a Loop but reorienting how you do business in a fundamental way. It is for anyone who wants to build a better relationship with customers and truly engage with them through a better model.

But before we can get to the good stuff, we need to better understand why marketing departments don't already have strong relationships with their customers. We need to evaluate what these departments are doing now and figure out why it might not be working.

And that means taking a closer look at the centerpiece of modern marketing: the Funnel.

CHAPTER 2

THE STORY OF THE FUNNEL, FROM F TO NULL

Human beings love models. Models help us make sense of the billions of data points that bombard our brains every minute. Models shape the way we think about the world. We adopt a model that seems to work and then we hold on to it until a better one comes along. Only then do we give up the old model—often kicking and screaming. And often very slowly.

The Funnel is a model that has been shaping our thinking about customer interactions for over a hundred years. But it originated in a world that no longer exists. The Funnel meshes beautifully with the world in which it was born. But the world has moved on.

And yet the model persists.

Let's take a very brief look at the origins of the Funnel and the world it was designed to reflect.

A Product of the Industrial Revolution

A basic premise we can all agree on is that companies have two core functions: they *produce* a product or service, and they *sell* that product or service. Production and sales. Around the turn of the twentieth century, the commerce world was busily trying to understand the mechanics of both of these functions so it could create standardized and optimized processes.

It was at this time—the late 1800s / early 1900s—that America really made the shift to a manufacturing-based economy. Prior to this, our country had been primarily agriculture based. Along with the shift to manufacturing came a greater focus on *processes*. Process became king. Ford started creating assembly lines to build the Model T, and businesses began to focus on concepts like scale, systems, efficiency, and throughput.

The essence of any manufacturing process was that you started with a bunch of raw material, you subjected it to a step-by-step modification process, and you ended up with a product. You lost some material and energy along the way, sure, but you ended up with something more valuable as a result.

The process was linear. It flowed in one direction. If you could tweak the process, gaining efficiency and eliminating waste along the way, you could increase your profitability and scalability. But essentially, the process was the process: start with a big pile of wheat plants, whittle it down to kernels, mill the kernels into flour, turn the flour into dough, bake the dough into loaves, pack the loaves into bags, and ship them.

So it's not surprising, against this backdrop, that the business world would try to develop a similar process for helping sales teams bring in customers—a process that could be as predictable, scalable, and replicable as the manufacturing process was.

IT STARTED WITH ADVERTISING

Toward the end of the 1800s, an advertising pro named E. St. Elmo Lewis proposed the notion that engaging readers follows a predictable process from Awareness to Interest to Desire. He later added Action as a fourth step (and the AIDA acronym was born). He was trying to teach people how to write better advertising for publications and periodicals in the preradio era.

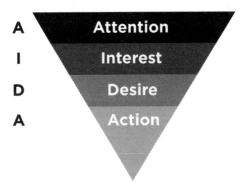

In 1924, a gentleman from the investment banking industry named William Townsend wrote a book called *Bond Salesmanship* to help salesmen sell financial instruments. He recognized that those same AIDA components could be used by salespeople to sell products, and he shaped them into the visual concept of a Funnel. He was the first person who proposed that AIDA could be a system: If you can make people *aware* of your product or service, you can generate *interest*. Interest leads to desire. Desire leads to *action*—i.e., a purchase.

Put another way: you start with a population of potential purchasers. By generating market awareness of your product or service, you create "suspects." Suspects then become "prospects," which are then converted into customers.

Using the Funnel model, sellers were advised to take the following standard steps:

Stage I. Secure attention.

Stage II. Hold attention through interest.

Stage III. Arouse desire.

Stage IV. Create confidence and belief.

Stage V. Secure decision and action.

Stage VI. Create satisfaction.[1]

In the early 1960s, authors Lavidge and Steiner proposed a "hierarchy of effects" that potential customers go through. These effects progress from Cognitive (think) to Affective (feel) to Behavioral (do) and include six stages:

---

1   Kim Majali, "How to Attract a Customer with a Marketing Model AIDA?," Europe IT Outsourcing, December 12, 2018, https://europeitoutsourcing.com/blog/marketing/attract-customer-marketing-model-aida/.

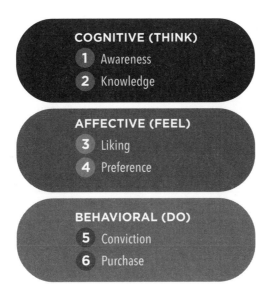

There have been countless variations and tweaks of these stages. Some Funnel models have three stages, some have four, some have six, some have seven, but they all describe essentially the same process. You start with a given market. You create awareness of your product. From there, you build interest. Once you've identified an interested party, you try to engage them, to get them to consider you. If that works, you try to influence them to make a decision in your favor. You close the sale, you ring the bell, you do it all over again.

FACTORY THINKING

The Funnel model reflects factory-style thinking because it's a predictable, repeatable process, and it's all about the numbers.

Essentially, the Funnel can be boiled down to one basic equation:

(Number of leads) x *(percentage rate of yield)* = *number of sales*

Each step in the process produces a certain yield rate, and at the end of the process, you get a final yield. For example:

- Out of every one hundred leads, thirty result in an encounter with a salesperson (30 percent yield).

- Out of all those encounters, four out of ten lead to a salesperson making an official pitch to a potential buyer (40 percent yield).

- Out of every five pitches to potential buyers, one results in a sale (20 percent yield).

The final yield rate in this example is 2.4 percent. If the process is reliable, it can be counted on to generate a predictable number of sales from a given number of leads. If you want more sales, you hire more salespeople to generate more leads. You pour those leads through your Funnel, you get your results. That's why big companies like IBM and Procter & Gamble taught the Funnel-selling method for decades.

KNOCK ON ENOUGH DOORS

I saw the Funnel in action growing up. My parents were both teachers who later went into sales. One of the products they sold was encyclopedia sets—which back in the day were actual, physical books and represented a sizable investment for a family. The process was a perfect illustration of the Funnel. A company like World Book Childcraft would create general awareness of its products by advertising. Then someone like my parents would ring doorbells and ask the adult resident who answered the door if they were interested in education for their children. A certain percentage would say yes. The salesperson would then say, "May I come in for a few minutes and talk to you about it?" Again, a certain percentage would say yes.

A formal presentation would then ensue. The in-house presentation, in turn, produced an average yield rate.

If you knocked on a hundred doors a day and you had a well-honed script, you could count on a certain number of sales at the end of a month or a year. *Day-to-day* sales might vary, but over time, predictable outcomes would occur. And so, on a company level, World Book Childcraft knew that if it had x number of warm bodies out there knocking on doors, it could sell y sets of encyclopedias.

Again, very factorylike. If you start off with enough raw material (homeowners, in this case) and you apply a good, consistent-quality process, you will get a certain predictable amount of output at the end. The more raw material you feed in and the more capacity you add to the process—e.g., hiring more sales reps—the more you can sell.

For better or worse, that was how things operated in the preinternet days. The reason the Funnel was a serviceable model was that the seller essentially controlled the whole process. The seller had the information and the means of distribution. The consumer's job was to consume what the seller was selling. Or not. The customer didn't have a lot of control over the process.

Marketing Gets Pulled In

The Funnel began to be stretched and pushed in new ways when marketing became responsible for driving revenue. This shift started happening in the late '90s / early '00s. Before that time, as I've mentioned, marketing was pretty much responsible only for art and brand stuff—doing shows, launching products, making tchotchkes. Marketing was a *cost* center for companies.

But as the internet became more and more prevalent, business stories began rapidly changing. By the early '00s, Google was only a few years old and Facebook was still a gleam in Mark Zuckerberg's eye, but buying and selling behavior was already transforming. Things were getting more complicated for sales teams. Customers were coming in from new channels and in new ways. So there was a shift. Marketing had better access to some of those channels and was now asked to do its part and fill the top of the Funnel with leads. And so it did.

Through marketing campaigns, online advertising, email—and through some of the older methods that were still in play, like phone calling and direct mailing—marketing started bringing leads to sales, but it was still a volume play—i.e., *if we can bring in enough leads at the top of the Funnel, sales can close a certain percentage of them, and we'll still come out ahead.*

It didn't take long for sales to realize that many of these marketing leads—especially the autogenerated ones—were garbage. The attitude was, "What are you doing, Marketing? You couldn't find a lead to hit the broad side of a barn. We need you to bring us people who aren't just breathing but who might actually want to buy our stuff. We need *qualified* leads." So by the middle of the '00s, marketing fell under pressure to start generating qualified leads.

That was when a concept called lead scoring started to resonate. At the time, I worked for Eloqua, the company that pioneered lead scoring, and I was on the team that developed it. Lead scoring was a system that rated the *quality* of leads according to a number of factors and assigned them a score. By using lead scoring and similar techniques, marketing gained a little more control of the quality of leads it sent to sales. Which, in theory, meant close rates should go up. And they did, to some extent. Marketing was putting more quality-control steps on the assembly line, but the process was still following the factory model.

In short, even after marketing became involved, the Funnel persisted. At the top of the Funnel, you were still trying to generate interest and engagement, at the middle of the Funnel, you were still qualifying leads, and at the bottom, you were still closing the customer.

A Sirius Decision

Then in the early 2000s, a company called Sirius Decisions was founded by some smart people at Gartner, the global research and advisory firm.

Recognizing some of the weaknesses of the Funnel, Sirius redesigned the model to reflect and track some of the new ways leads were coming in and to establish a new set of standards for the process. Their model took into account the fact that both marketing and sales now bring in leads and do so in a number of different ways. Buyers come in at different points, and there are different ways to qualify that demand. Sirius coined terms such as Marketing Qualified Lead (MQL), Sales Qualified Lead (SQL), and Sales Accepted Lead (SAL), which we all now use. Sirius called its new-and-improved Funnel the Demand Waterfall.

The Sirius folks also added a lot more benchmarking to the Funnel. Marketing and sales teams ate this up. They could now find out how they were doing compared to industry standards. So, for example, if the industry standard for MQL was 30 percent, then your team should be at 30 percent or better. And if you were doing better than 30 percent, you could tell your boss you were doing a great job with your marketing.

Sirius Decisions then built a wide range of products and services around its model, offering trainings, consultations, and information packages at various fee levels. Essentially, Sirius offered to help your company achieve market dominance through competitive benchmarking.

But in order for that benchmarking to matter, and in order for the team at Sirius to establish dominance of its own, Sirius needed to transform its model into an industry standard.

And it did. The Waterfall caught on pretty quickly.

In short order, Sirius Decisions established itself as the ultimate authority on best practices for marketing and sales. And that's still the case today. While there are many models out there, the vast majority of them are Waterfall clones, all operating from the same core assumptions. The Waterfall has been revised a couple of times, but it's still the eight-hundred-pound gorilla.

But It's Still a Funnel

The problem is, the Waterfall isn't really working. That's no slight on the Sirius team. As a company, Sirius offers its clients a lot of useful information and analysis, but its core model isn't really delivering for a lot of companies. Although the Waterfall adds specificity and structure to the Funnel, that specificity can actually be a problem. For many companies, the model is too rigid to be implemented. Many companies can't implement it at all.

Benchmarking has become problematic too. Benchmarking against multiple companies and within your own company gets harder and harder as the customer keeps changing and companies keep changing and as you bring in different product lines, different sales teams, different pricing models, and different market conditions. Benchmarked standards would work beautifully if life took place in a vacuum, in a perfectly controlled test environment. But alas, that's not how business works.

The fact is, there's no absolute truth or certainty to be had when it comes to modeling sales and marketing. While Sirius's model may have reflected how *some* businesses worked, it doesn't reflect how *all* businesses work. It doesn't even reflect how *most* businesses work. In fact, after two decades in this industry, I have yet to encounter a single company that has been able to fully adopt and operationalize the Waterfall without collapsing in on itself first.

And that's a huge problem. Why? Because marketing departments are relying on these Funnels to turn them into revenue centers. In the next chapter, I'll tell you *why* that strategy has been failing and why it's probably never going to work. Then we'll figure out what we can do about it.

> **I have yet to encounter a single company that has been able to fully adopt and operationalize the Waterfall without collapsing in on itself first.**

CHAPTER 3

NEWTON'S LIE

B ack in chapter 1, we asked, *Why don't our organizations love us?* Answering that question was easy: it's because we marketers aren't seen as revenue-earners. We're seen as cost centers; an expense of doing business, not a revenue contributor.

So how do we change that perception? Well, to start bringing in more revenue, we need to understand why we *aren't* bringing in revenue now. And, as we saw earlier, that requires us to reevaluate our relationship with the people who *provide* the revenue: our customers.

Ideally, of course, we all *want* our customers/clients to have a good experience with our company—no one gets up in the morning and says, "Hmm, how can I make my customers miserable today?"

But often the effect is that the customer *does* have a poor experience. Why?

Because we're busy thinking about *our* systems, *our* technology, *our* campaigns, *our* reports, *our* data, *our* processes, not the customer. Because our systems and processes are based on a model that doesn't take the customer into account: the Funnel.

The Funnel *has never* really addressed the customer's experience, but in the old days, when the seller controlled the whole purchase experience, we could get away with using it. We can't get away with it anymore. It just doesn't work.

A Flawed Premise

How do I know the Funnel/Waterfall isn't working? Because I receive phone calls from my marketing clients, literally on a daily basis, saying things like:

"This doesn't represent my business. This is not how my customers buy."

"The model's too rigid."

"It doesn't make sense to me. I can't use an arbitrary approach like this."

"I need different Funnels. I need different approaches for my different product lines."

"I'm not achieving these numbers. I don't know how they get the numbers they're claiming."

"Our sales and marketing teams still aren't aligned. I put the Funnel in place, and that hasn't brought us closer together."

"I've implemented part of the Funnel, but I can't get other parts of it to work."

"I understand what I'm *supposed* to do—I just don't know how to do it in my environment with my systems and my processes and my people."

"I get the broader concept, and I like the Waterfall in theory. But how do I make it work in my environment?"

Maybe the problem isn't with the user; maybe it's with the model itself.

IMPROVING THE MOUSETRAP

The issue with models, as I said in the last chapter, is that they become so engrained in our thinking that it takes us a while to notice they're no longer reflecting the world as it is. In many ways, the Funnel has been like the wheel. It has been so basic to our thinking, we've never thought to question it. Especially when people—like the good folks at Sirius—keep tweaking it to make it better. First someone adds rubber to the wheel. The wheel works better! Then someone adds bearings, then shocks, and the wheel works even better. But it's still a wheel. Which is great—unless the world has switched to using flying skateboards.

To use another metaphor: improvements to the Funnel have all been attempts to build a better mousetrap. But what if we've now discovered that mice are an intelligent species and we want to have a relationship with them instead of stomping them out?

FOR WHOM ARE FUNNELS MADE?

To understand why the Funnel is fundamentally incapable of fostering strong relationships between marketers and customers, we need to understand how the Funnel was built—specifically, from whose point of view it was built.

Think about the intrinsic metaphor here. Think about Funnels. The operating principle on which they work is *gravity*. The Funnel system assumes there is a force that pulls customers down from a state of ignorance to a state of purchase. It's about volume and velocity.

The Funnel is essentially an assembly-line process born from an assembly-line mindset. It's unidirectional and transactional. You plug in raw material at the top of the line, and you get output at the bottom. And you're done. You pack it, you ship it, you never see the raw material or the item again. Your relationship with the customer— such as it was—is over.

If you want better results, well, you can try to improve the factory process. Maybe put in some better quality controls, train your delivery drivers better, use cheaper materials, improve your tracking technology. But still your orientation toward the customer hasn't changed. You're still not seeing the customer in terms of relationship. You're seeing them in terms of a transaction.

The Funnel is transactional. It serves and reflects *our* needs but has little to do with what the customer is experiencing and desiring. Furthermore, it is based on the illusion that the seller still controls the marketing, selling, and sales processes. And that is no longer true.

The Customer Is Playing a Different Game—Chutes and Ladders

If we were to study our customers' experiences, we would see they're playing a different game entirely. Far from following a Funnel-like process in making a purchasing decision, the customer plays a game that looks more like Chutes and Ladders. This has always been the case, really, but it is vastly more true in the internet era, where the customer has control of the process.

SALE

From a customer's perspective, a decision to buy a product or service follows a "process" that can go up and down, sideways, backward, and/or diagonally. Two steps up the ladder, one steps sideways, then back down the chute. It is anything but linear.

With small purchases, such as grocery items, the process may be fairly straightforward, but when it comes to larger purchases—things that have an emotional aspect or that people need to save or plan for— all bets are off. For example, the customer might be getting ready to buy a car or remodel their kitchen, but then their water heater breaks or the family breadwinner gets laid off, and they have to postpone that purchase. Or perhaps they're in the market for a piano, but their kid takes up violin instead. Or maybe they've decided to start shopping for a boat *now*, but they're not really planning to buy the boat until five years later, when they retire.

We try to pull customers "down the chute" toward us, but instead they move *up* a ladder, make a lateral move, come down a different ladder, and so on due to an infinite variety of factors—some of which we may be able to influence and others that have nothing to do with us at all. How can a simple unidirectional model like the Funnel address such a reality?

It can't.

What the Funnel Misses

The Funnel still catches *some* customers and purchases, of course, but it is missing more and more of them. That's because both businesses and customers are changing rapidly in the new economy. Here are just a few of today's customer realities that the Funnel fails to address …

THE CUSTOMER IS NOW IN CONTROL

As internet commerce has ballooned, the customer has been gaining more and more control over the purchase cycle. Customers can now research our products inside out and backward, learn about our weaknesses as vendors, and find competitive products at the best prices on the planet. In 1990, customers had maybe 5 percent control over their purchase cycle. Now they're controlling almost all of it. And they're 60, 70, 80 percent of the way into the purchase cycle before our company even knows about it. They can essentially air-drop onto our assembly line at any point and say, "Hi! I'm here, serve me." You're worrying about optimizing your Funnel, and your customer is saying, "I'm not even *using* your Funnel, bro."

NEW CHANNELS ARE ACCELERATING

New communication channels are popping up constantly. Social media, for instance, is a channel we didn't even have fifteen years ago. Now it's massive. Smartphones are now ubiquitous; we didn't have them as a channel even *ten* years ago. Folks are surfing the web, banking, grocery shopping, and watching movies on their phones. There's a constant parade of new apps, like Instagram, Snapchat, and TikTok, that rise and fall in popularity. Different age groups and demographics respond to marketing and sales differently on all these platforms. My dad still goes down to the deli every morning and gets his newspaper. I get my news on my smartphone. As marketers, we no longer pull customers into *our* Funnel; we have to go to *them* where *they* are.

CUSTOMERS ARE UNIQUE

No matter how much data you collect, it is extremely difficult to predict exactly how a customer will behave. Two people might have exactly the same politics and agree on every issue, but one might vote by mail, the other in person—different voting behaviors. A husband and wife might share the same taste in movies and TV shows but might read very different types of books. There are so many factors that influence how an individual customer buys. If you're trying to use a rigid system like a Funnel, you just won't be fluid enough to capture this.

YOU'RE SELLING TO MORE THAN ONE PERSON

Customers are usually part of a team. That team might be a couple, a family, or a work unit. Often sales and marketing people fail to realize that although they're dealing with a single customer, they're actually selling to the customer's whole team. Nothing drives my wife crazier, for example, than having a salesperson assume that I'm making the decisions (because I'm the man) and addressing their whole pitch to me. That's a sure way to blow a sale. If I'm talking to a realtor about buying a house, that realtor had better find out about my *whole family's* needs.

In business-to-business services (B2B), you might do a great job marketing and selling to your point person in a company, but you may not realize they have five other people on their team. And those team members may have relationships with other vendors. The Funnel doesn't help you understand that there are five peers you need to build a relationship with. You might wine and dine your one identified customer and do all the right things, but then at the end of the month, you might get the dreaded phone call, "Sorry, but the team has decided to go in a different direction."

THE CUSTOMER ONLY WANTS ONE PRODUCT RIGHT NOW, BUT ...

How often have you tried to buy a single product and the salesperson tries to sell you everything in their product line? Customers aren't interested in product lines, they want the product they need now, period. If I'm buying a garden hose at Home Depot, I don't care if there's a sale on lumber. I might need lumber six months from now, but I don't need it now. Customers do have a lifetime value, but all that value can't be realized *today*.

On the other hand, customers do have complex and multiple needs over the long haul. And if we take the time to get to know them, we can sell them a lot more. Take two customers who walk into that same Home Depot. Each buys a gallon of paint. From a Funnel perspective, that's a hundred percent conversion rate, end of story. But these customers might be very different. One might just be repainting a dingy room, the other might be adding details to an antique house he's just bought. This second person might need new cabinets, new lighting fixtures, new toilets, new flooring … And if we paid attention to the signals, we could sell them a lot more.

Clients, Not Customers

There's a universal solution to all of these problems, and that is to stop thinking of customers as one-off transactions and learn to develop *relationships* with them. Customers can only be "leads" at the top of our Funnel once, but they can be *clients* forever. And that's the way we need to think of customers—as clients.

There is a huge difference between customers and clients. A customer is someone with whom we execute a sales transaction; a client is someone we get to know as a unique human being, someone with a set of needs and life situations that unfold over time. A client is someone we stay in touch and try to serve in many different ways as their lives and needs change.

A customer represents a onetime or sporadic purchase. A client is someone with whom we plan to do repeat business over the years— not only repeat purchases of the same product but also new products and services that emerge as the client's needs change and evolve. A client is someone with whom we have a *relationship*. A client trusts us, asks us for advice, calls us when they have questions. A client has friends and family members we may be able to serve.

Obviously, we don't develop client relationships for every kind of sale. A customer who buys a notebook in an office supply store is just making a onetime purchase. There's no ongoing relationship with the notebook manufacturer. But the *office supply store* that sells the notebook can and should view the customer as a potential client, one with a wide variety of needs that will change over the years.

***

Marketing departments work so hard, investing so much time, energy, and creativity in their work, that when our customers don't meet us halfway, we often feel inclined to blame *them*. We feel like our customers are missing something. But our customers aren't missing anything. *We* are. We're missing their point of view. We've adopted an elaborate sales model that never once accounts for what our customers are actually experiencing.

In short, we've become narcissists. And the reason we don't have real relationships with our customers is because our customers have figured out something we still haven't: you can't have a relationship with a narcissist. In the next chapter, we'll see why narcissistic relationships never work, and we'll begin developing a game plan for wooing our customers back.

CHAPTER 4

BECAUSE WE DON'T LOVE THEM

S o we've determined that we need to foster a closer relationship with our customers. And that means becoming truly customer centric and, whenever possible, turning our customers into clients. If we can get our customers/ clients to love us, our companies will begin to love us too because of the new revenue we'll be bringing in.

So that raises another question: Why don't our customers love us now?

Fundamentally, it's because we don't love them. We think we do, but often we're more focused on our own needs. It's kind of like a dating situation: *I like you, I want to hang out with you, but I'm not willing to put your needs before my own.*

That's not real love. That's narcissism. Our marketing mechanisms are fundamentally narcissistic.

In this chapter, we're going to take a closer look at how narcissism fails to serve the needs of the customer and, ultimately, fails to serve our own needs as a result.

And along the way, we're going to begin to discover the path toward a new model—one that fosters strong bonds between our clients and ourselves, as well as between our departments and the rest of our organizations.

Narcissism

Narcissism. Think about what it is. It's a pathological failure to see beyond ourselves—our own wants and needs. It's about using people to get what *we* want and then ignoring them when we think they have nothing left to offer us. It's about treating people as a means to an end—ours—rather than as complex human beings with evolving needs, desires, and experiences.

NARCISSISM IS PUSHY

A narcissistic approach is one that pushes *our* agenda—namely, to sell a product—on others. But people have a fundamentally negative attitude toward being pushed. It's an instinctual thing. Try this if you don't believe me: ask someone to hold their hands up with their palms facing you. Now place your palms on theirs and push. The other person will automatically push back.

Pushing triggers push*back*, conflict. It happens reflexively.

No one enjoys being pounced on by a salesperson the instant they walk in the door of a store or onto the lot of a car dealership. No one enjoys being phoned at dinner by telemarketers. That's why people have two essential reactions to being pushed; they either push back or they avoid the encounter entirely.

Not long ago customers were *forced* to endure the car salesmen, the door-to-door vacuum sellers, and the cold calling because that was the only way they could access the products they needed. But nowadays customers are in control of the sales process and their attitude is "Don't sell to me, don't try to convince me, don't bombard me with content that doesn't fit my needs right now. Educate me, share your knowledge, and help me navigate my journey on *my* terms, and *I'll* tell *you* when I'm ready to have the sales conversation."

NARCISSISM IS NEEDY

Narcissism also has a needy quality, that underlying sense of "I need to make this sale because I need to make my sales quota" or "I need to earn my bonus" and so on. Marketing exhibits this behavior too. When we blast out campaign after campaign in a relentless pursuit to drive more leads, we are only thinking about ourselves. Everyone finds neediness repellent. As an example, look at the lonely guy who cruises the nightspots trying desperately to meet women. Women run the other way. His neediness broadcasts itself like a ninety-megawatt radio tower.

When people sense a needy, selfish agenda, they regard everything we do as an effort to manipulate them into saying yes to us. And they're right.

NARCISSISM IS DISHONEST

In a narcissistic relationship, we often *say* we want to serve the customer, and we may even make efforts in that direction, but we don't really have their needs in mind. We are serving ourselves. If we really cared about our customers, we would offer them the advice and information *they* really need, even if this meant possibly losing out on a short-term sale.

Politics, sad to say, is a good example of a dishonest relationship. Most politicians—on both sides of the fence—say they care about their constituents, but they really care about staying in office and protecting their parties' interests. They may pay lip service to "serving the people," but all of their behavior is motivated toward getting reelected and securing "wins" for their party.

The Funnel Is Pro-Narcissism

The Funnel is a model that supports and advances a narcissistic point of view. Again, it's based on an assembly-line mindset. It focuses on throughput, volume, and velocity—mass-production elements. If we add more prospects at the top, we can improve our conversion points at the bottom. Presto, more revenue.

The Funnel is a tool companies use to optimize performance, much like ROI calculators, strategic planning tools, and spreadsheets. It's detached and quantitative. It has been a useful mechanism for over a hundred years, but it's not about the customer at all. It's about the company. It does not even contain a structure for communicating with customers. It does not ask whether or not our brand promises are being fulfilled, whether the customer's expectations are being met, or whether the customer is getting value from our products.

The Funnel puts us in a *taking*-oriented perspective, not a *giving*-oriented one.

The Funnel process ends when the bell is rung. Its unspoken message is, "This activity is over the moment my needs are met." See how far that attitude will get you in a marriage.

Love Is the Answer

If we want our customers to love us, we must love them—which we can't do from a narcissistic framework.

What does it mean to love our customers? Well, obviously, it doesn't mean we're going to become intimately involved with each of them. But love really is a good word to get us thinking in the right direction. A simple definition of love is to put another person's needs ahead of our own—or at least on par with our own. Practically speaking, that means caring about what the other person is experiencing, learning what their preferences are, and helping them get their needs met.

Love means being proactive instead of reactive. Many companies put *reactive* measures in place and mistake this for being customer centric. They send out customer satisfaction surveys and offer "customer service" numbers to call when something goes wrong. Or a college, for example, might assign each student an advisor they can see if they want to and establish a "crisis office" students can visit if they're having problems. But these are reactive methods.

Loving our customers is a proactive perspective. It means asking, *How is your experience so far? What do you need? How can I help?*

It requires an effort to see things from the customer's point of view.

> **Loving our customers requires an effort to see things from the customer's point of view.**

When we do that, when we really try to find out what kind of experience *they're* having, we discover several things about our customers:

CUSTOMERS DON'T WANT TO BE ON AN ASSEMBLY LINE

Customers have zero interest in being treated like widgets on our assembly line. They dislike being thought of as numbers. Also, they don't want to go down the assembly line the same way everybody else does; they want to make purchases in a way that suits *them*. Chutes and Ladders, remember? Maybe they want to buy our services piecemeal, not as part of the package we're selling. Maybe they need us only for the final stages of their project. Maybe their process is such that they *can't* go down our line. As customers acquire more control over the buying process, the Funnel/assembly-line model becomes less and less relevant.

CUSTOMERS WANT CHOICE

Today's customers want choice, even with small purchases. They don't want their choices dictated, like in the old days. I was in the supermarket the other day and counted thirty-two separate Oreo SKUs. There are probably more. When I was a kid, there was one.

When it comes to larger and more meaningful purchases, customers want customization options. But here's an important point. They don't necessarily want *unlimited* options either. When they are given too many options, they can become overwhelmed and go into brain lock. They usually prefer a tastefully and intelligently curated set of choices. Buying a home in a planned development is a good example. The builder might offer four different home models, a choice of lots, and a menu of options for floor tiles, kitchen counters, cabinets, plumbing fixtures, etc. Customers are okay with a house that's 50 percent mass-produced, 50 percent customized, because they don't want the hassle and expense of building a 100 percent customized house. The trade-off gives them the best of both worlds.

CUSTOMERS CHOOSE FROM EMOTION

When customers are shopping for any major purchase, they make their decision from a place of emotion, backed up by logic. Surprisingly, many of us miss this point. We assume that when it comes to the big things, customers rely on reason primarily. So we bombard prospective customers with logical selling points, but we don't get in there at the level where the decision is really being made.

Again, house shopping is a good example. You and your spouse might sit down together, figure out a mortgage you can afford, and discuss a whole host of considerations for your new home, such as number of bedrooms, school district, and nearness to work. But often it's an emotional reaction—such as the feeling you get standing by the apple tree in the backyard—that moves you to pull the trigger, to maybe even spend more money than you planned. You then circle back and justify the purchase logically: "It's a good investment. It's more than we wanted to spend, but we'll do a thirty-year mortgage instead of a twenty-five."

College choice is another example. My kids are college age now, and my wife and I have done a lot of campus visits with them. There are a thousand practical considerations that go into choosing a school, but usually the decision comes down to "This place feels right. I could see myself here," not "I looked at the twenty-year rate of return on job placement and salary versus cost, and my financial analysis tells me this is the best school."

Only by having a *relationship* with a customer do we get a glimpse into their unique emotional perspective.

CUSTOMERS WANT TO BE SEEN AND HEARD

Customers (all human beings, actually) have a fundamental desire to be recognized, acknowledged, and appreciated. Some of the easiest and most effective things we can do to make a connection with customers/clients are to simply reach out to them at various points in the purchasing and postpurchasing processes, offer them resources and a listening ear to help them make a decision (without "selling"), welcome them and thank them for coming aboard, ask them how their early experience is going, and find out if they need any help installing or learning to use our products. Most of all, *listen* to whatever they tell us. And show them we heard them by taking some form of action.

Toward a Better Model

For years, sales and marketing departments have subscribed to the Funnel model of managing customer development. And it hasn't gotten us closer to our customers; it's moved us further away. That's because the Funnel model isn't built with the customer in mind. It isn't even built with *us* in mind.

It's rigid. It's nonresponsive. It's benchmarked against companies that are nothing like ours. It treats the customer journey like a straight, gravitationally powered line, when in fact the customer journey goes up, down, sideways, and diagonally. It assumes the customer relationship is identical across our brand, when actually the relationship differs from product to product. And, most important of all, it assumes the relationship ends at close of deal.

That's like saying a marriage ends on the wedding day.

That customer—the one who has progressed past being a "lead"—isn't *dead*. They're still alive, and they're actually *using* our product or service now. Which means that they could potentially have a closer, more rewarding relationship with us than ever before. They could become advocates for us. They could renew their purchase or buy another product.

And yet we ignore all of that. No matter how much of our company's revenue might come from existing customers (or could if we let it), we devote most of our time, money, and energy to generating new leads. At best, perhaps we reach back out to existing customers when it's time to renew, or we send them satisfaction surveys. This isn't only a poor way to treat people, it's also bad business. We're investing money into these relationships and then abandoning them.

As a consequence of this behavior, we aren't able to deliver the revenue we'd like to. Which, in turn, results in failures of authority, credibility, and job security within our companies.

At the beginning of this chapter, I asked: *Why don't our customers love us?* And I think the answer is clear now: because *we don't love them.*

But it doesn't have to be that way. We can adopt another kind of model: one that accounts for the realities of the customer experience; one that has no end point; one that can adapt to the unique characteristics of our individual organizations.

Part II will show us how ...

PART II
WELCOME TO THE LOOP

CHAPTER 5

THE LOOP

I n part I, we saw how Funnels facilitate bad relationships between marketers and customers.

That dynamic leads to a shortage of revenue, which, in turn, undermines the relationship between marketers and the organizations they serve.

But it wouldn't be correct to say that Funnels are wrong or fundamentally bad. Rather, they are *incomplete*. Because they're built from the perspective of sellers, they model only half of the customer experience—from ignorance to purchase. But in many ways, purchase is only the *beginning* of the customer's experience. In many ways, too, it is only the beginning of the customer *relationship*.

Here in part II, we're going to look at the rest of the customer experience and learn how it can be modeled. We're going to discover *the Loop*.

"Discovering" the Loop

First of all, I can't say that we at TPG were literally the first team to come up with a Loop concept. But we were one of the earliest to identify it and start using it. And we arrived at it through our own authentic, organic process.

We set out to devise a model that would represent the *entire* customer/client experience. And we began with the previous insight: that Funnels aren't wrong about everything—they're just incomplete. They have immense practical value, but they tell only half the story.

So as we gathered around the trusty whiteboard, we started out by drawing the Funnel exactly as it is—vertical, upright, gravity-based. And then we started asking ourselves questions such as, *But there's so much stuff we do after close. Shouldn't the Funnel keep going? We filter leads down to a close, but now we want to* expand *the business, right? Shouldn't the Funnel radiate back* outward *once the client comes in?*

So the next thing we did was to draw kind of a reverse Funnel coming out the bottom. We attached a triangle going the other way. The thing now looked like an hourglass. And we started thinking about the steps that occur before, during, and after the sale. The hourglass model made more sense to us but still wasn't quite what we wanted. So we started questioning, *Why gravity? That makes it seem like customers flow magically from the top to the close and that they just keep flowing and expanding by some natural force.* That didn't make sense because we knew there was a lot of work that had to be done to grow the client.

We concluded the vertical orientation didn't reflect what was actually happening. So we said, *Let's turn it on its side.* That orientation seemed truer. But still it felt like an assembly line—you feed people in from the left and they spit out on the right. It didn't reflect the idea that customers are in the process all the time and might be at multiple stages simultaneously.

A Funnel, regardless of which direction it's pointed in, still feels unidirectional. We wanted something that was multidirectional. That was when we realized our drawing looked like a figure-eight racetrack. So we smoothed out the curves, and suddenly we realized we'd created … an infinity loop. A continuous flow.

Now, *that* felt right. The Loop had arrived.

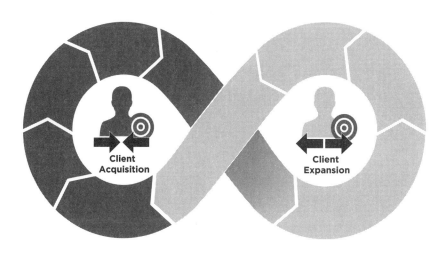

We realized that one side of the Loop looked like the traditional Funnel but with some notable differences. You still go through certain predictable steps to acquire a customer/client (although we wanted to build a better experience on that side too). But actions, processes, behaviors, and content had to change so as to become customer centric, not company centric. That became, for us, the Client Acquisition side of the Loop.

We knew the other side had to be about Client Expansion and that that side had to explore in much more rigor all the things that happen after the sale. So we identified several concrete steps on that side of the Loop too.

We'll look at all those steps in a moment. But first let's appreciate why we liked our new model better.

Why the Loop?

The Loop, like the Funnel, is just an abstract model. It is not meant to be slavishly adhered to or taken too literally. That said, it represents a quantum leap beyond the Funnel, and it can shape our thinking and our behavior in much more productive ways.

INFINITY IS THE WAY

The Loop represents infinity, which is a good way of looking at customer/client relationships. They are—or ought to be—perennial, not dead-ended, not finite.

An infinity loop captures the nature of relationships in general. A relationship is constantly changing, constantly renewing itself, constantly evolving, constantly waxing and waning in intensity. But it keeps going; it doesn't stop.

A relationship such as a marriage goes through phases, ups, and downs. It is not rainbows and roses every day. There are arguments. There is suffering and pain. But there's also love and commitment and trust. There are times of greater closeness, times of greater distance. There are seasons. Your marriage is not the same ten, twenty, or thirty years into it as it was when you first got married. Your needs change, your maturity level changes, your circumstances change—so the marriage must be renewed and reinvigorated again and again.

Your relationship with your client is the same way. It changes. The client changes over time. Their needs change, their resources change. Different people in the company or family start to use your products and services. Your company changes too. It changes its messaging, its brand, its packaging; it offers new products and services.

So you and the client are constantly in flux. That's why it is important to check in with the client regularly and find out how they're doing and what they need. They may be at a place where they need a whole new range of products and services from you, but you wouldn't know it if you were just transactionally focused. Relationships must be nurtured and renewed.

IT'S A HOLISTIC, NOT A SILOED, APPROACH

Some of us sell just one service or one product, but many of us are in businesses that sell more than one. And so of course we want our clients to buy more products from us. But the Funnel isn't set up for that. The Funnel looks at every new transaction as a restart at the top of the Funnel, as a new lead. And that colors the way we treat our clients/customers.

When we treat an existing customer as if they're a new lead, that results in an awkward and annoying experience for the customer. It's like when you go into a doctor's office and they say, "Tell me about your history," and your reaction is, "I just gave it to someone in the other room. And by the way, I've been coming here for fifteen years, can't you look it up in my chart?"

As a customer, you probably find yourself often asking: *Why am I filling out another form? Why do I have to give my personal information to three different people on the same phone call? Why are you trying to sell me a product I bought three years ago?* The answer to these questions is: because the company treats every department, every product, as its own silo. The business is not built around the customer and is not even cognizant of who its own customers are and what they're going through.

Treating existing customers this way is not only insulting to the customer, it is a failure to maximize the customer relationship. That's not to say you can't have different sales teams for different product lines, but each salesperson should, at minimum, look up the customer in the customer relationship management system and find out they've purchased multiple other products in the past. The salesperson could then at least say, "Hey, Michelle, thanks so much for being a great client of ABC. I know your company has purchased multiple products from us in the past … "

Maintaining a deep and real relationship with the client is even better. When we do that, we can oversee and even coordinate all the different places where the client is at in regard to our products and maybe help them make some intelligent decisions.

IT'S FLEXIBLE, NOT RIGID

Even though we put ten "standard" stages in the Loop, the one thing we agreed upon from the start was that our model would be flexible. We knew a lot of people were having trouble with the Funnel or the Waterfall, saying, *But that's not my business. I don't have x number of stages in my Funnel. I have y stages in my Funnel.* Or *I have multiple Funnels. This model is not working for me, I'm having a hard time implementing it.* So the Loop is just a basic representation, not an absolute. If you need to have two stages on the left and seventeen on the right, no problem! What matters is knowing who your clients are and what they are experiencing—and knowing that you need to optimize both the acquisition and the expansion stages through an ongoing relationship. The rest can be customized to your business's specifics.

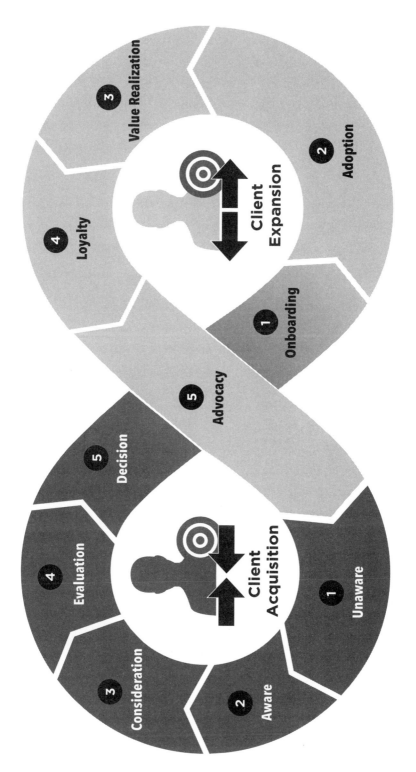

The Ten Stages

With the understanding that these stages are not written in stone, let's take a quick look at the "default" stages on each side of the Loop: five stages of Client Acquisition and five stages of Client Expansion.

You're probably generally familiar with the first five stages, as they correspond roughly to the Funnel model you've likely encountered in your career. What is different in the Loop is that we are now taking a customer-focused approach in these stages. That means our processes, our content, our actions, and our KPIs change as well. We'll take a brief look at them here.

THE FIVE STAGES OF CLIENT ACQUISITION

1. Unaware

This is the stage at which the potential customer/client does not even know they have a problem or a need yet. The car is running fine, the house is looking good, the phone is doing what it's supposed to do. The customer is happy where they're at.

None of us knew we needed a smartphone a few years ago; we were happy with our BlackBerrys. We didn't know we wanted GPS systems in our cars. We didn't know we wanted to deposit checks from our phones—until we became aware of these possibilities. At the Unaware stage, our job as marketers is to *create* awareness. We do this through education, brand building, storytelling, use cases, and more.

We try to move customers out of their comfort zone either by making them realize they have a problem (or soon will) or by creating an emotional connection to something they didn't know they wanted.

While some things are similar between the Funnel and the Loop in this stage, such as advertising and storytelling, there are some notable differences in the Loop. First we focus on building out a complete buying life cycle, including customers' personas, needs, and triggers, as well as sources of information. We do this so we can understand the *customer's* process before we model our own.

In the Funnel, we do not care about the customer's process—we care only about our assembly line. In the Loop, we take more time to research current challenges that potential clients are facing. We don't view marketing as the only entity to tell the story. Rather, we include multiple client-facing roles within our company—sales, service, channel partners—in addition to marketing. We collaborate and determine the best way to raise awareness while focusing on how we can help the potential client improve.

2. Aware

In this stage, as the name implies, the potential customer moves from a state of blissful (or miserable) ignorance to one of awareness of a need or desire. The car windshield cracks, the neighbor puts a swimming pool in their backyard, a new smartphone comes out with an awesome new feature. Suddenly the customer has a problem that needs solving or a new desire that needs fulfilling. They move from a state of vague potential to one of focused potential. There's a strong likelihood they're going to make a purchase.

Our goal here is not just to move clients down the assembly line to the next station. It is to help the client go to whatever step is next in *their* journey.

Building upon the buying life cycle from Unaware, we focus on content needs for each involved persona and determine what activities are needed from our customer-facing roles to deliver the best experience at this stage. Our goal here is not just to move clients down the assembly line to the next station. It is to help the client go to whatever step is next in *their* journey. We want to be a Sherpa, a guide.

3. Consideration

Here the customer starts to gather information and do research. They start googling swimming pools and reading reviews of smartphones and windshield repair companies. Maybe they go down to their local home store or start driving around neighborhoods to get a better idea of what the pool design options are. They're starting to get clear on the features and functions and size they want. They're zeroing in on a budget. They're narrowing their list of vendors.

In the Funnel, this is typically where we would ramp up sales activity, engaging in more aggressive tactics to get the prospect to a proposal or demo stage. In the Loop, we are continuing to act as a Sherpa, and we ask different questions. *What is my potential client concerned with? What information do they need to help with their consideration? How can I make this process easier for them?*

4. Evaluation

The customer is now doing some analysis and making some definitive business decisions on each product model and vendor on their short list. They're looking at case studies, detailed reviews. If they're a B2B customer, they're talking to analysts, doing financial calculations. They're getting their whole buying center involved in the decision, not just one or two people. Presentations and meetings are taking place. People are making arguments on behalf of their favored vendors. The team is moving toward a place of decision.

In the Funnel, we are countering objections. We are offering discounts or using aggressive sales tactics to drive to a close. In the Loop, we are helping the prospective client build their business case. We are making the decision process simpler by providing them the right information at the right time. We are helping them buy and make a decision on their terms, not ours.

5. Decision

This is the stage where we, as sellers and marketers, are trying to get the client to move over the line and make that commitment. Ideally, the client makes a firm decision and proceeds with the purchase. The B2B customer informs the vendor of their decision and starts formulating legal terms and conditions, doing contract negotiations, agreeing to terms, making plans, coming up with project timelines, securing funding/financing, getting stakeholder alignment, and so on. The contract is signed, and we now have a customer.

In the old Funnel model, our work was now done. The customer was handed off to the appropriate service and/or operations teams, and we started looking for new customers.

But in the Loop model, our customer relationship work is only getting started.

THE FIVE STAGES OF CLIENT EXPANSION

Client Expansion is the side of the Loop where we convert customers into satisfied users of our products and raving fans of our company. Here is where trust and loyalty are developed. Here is where we try to become the go-to solution for a whole range of client needs and desires.

We'll spend a chapter on each of these stages, so I'll introduce them only briefly here.

1. Onboarding

Often after the purchase is made, there is a silent period, a complete drop-off in customer-oriented activity. That's because we've used the traditional Funnel and consider our job done. From the client's point of view, though, they've just spent six months evaluating our company. They're excited to get going on all the stuff we promised. Suddenly their phone isn't ringing and they're wondering what happens next. *Onboarding* is our first and greatest opportunity to start building an ongoing and trusting relationship. During onboarding, we can welcome the customer, tell them what's coming next, hold their hand, answer their questions, and make them feel important and appreciated.

2. Adoption

Adoption is the next critical stage because if the customer doesn't actually adopt the product we've sold them, they're never going to feel they got good ROI, and the relationship will stall. The *degree* to which the customer is using our products and services is critically important. This isn't so important with a minor purchase, but if a client has paid three hundred thousand dollars for software and no one's using it—or they're using only a fraction of the features—that's a big problem. How can we begin to expect loyalty if the customer is not even getting usage of what they've already bought? Clients need a lot of communication at this stage.

3. Value Realization

Once the customer adopts the product/service and uses it for a while, they evaluate it. Did they get the value they were looking for and were promised? Did the utility of the product or service meet their expectations? Did it deliver even more value than they thought it would? Less?

4. Loyalty

If we've done a good job of onboarding the customer, ensuring adoption, and confirming value realization, then the customer is likely going to fall in love with our brand, our product, and our people. They're going to continue to buy from us again and again. And if we ask them to be a reference or to serve as a case study, they'll be delighted to help us.

5. Advocacy

Ideally, the customer will fall in love with us so deeply, they'll become an advocate for us. We won't even have to ask them anymore. They'll write blogs about us and recommend us to their friends just because they want other people to have the same quality experience they had. When you recommend a restaurant to a friend, you're not doing that because someone paid you. You're doing it because you had a valuable experience, and you want your friend to get that value too. Advocacy is the holy grail of Customer Expansion.

The beauty of the Loop is that it facilitates a constant departure *from* and return *to* the acquisition phase. There's **internal return**: clients in the loyalty phase come back to renew or buy from us again and again. And there's **external return**: clients in the loyalty and advocacy phase help us acquire new customers.

***

By reflecting the customer's actual experience and by reminding us of the various ways we can stay involved with the customer, the Loop works to ensure that we will build closer relationships with our customers.

Although at first glance the Loop might appear to have the same rigidity for which we criticized the Funnel, that's not the case. In part III, we'll talk about how the Loop can adapt to reflect all of the many organic variations between different types of companies, customers, and products.

But first let's go deep and take a closer look at the five stages of Client Expansion.

CHAPTER 6

ONBOARDING

 few stats to chew on as we dive into the concept of onboarding:

- Acquiring new customers is between five and twenty-five times more expensive than retaining existing ones.[2]

- Sixty-three percent of customers give consideration to the company's onboarding program when making a purchasing decision.[3]

---

2   Khalid Saleh, "Customer Acquisition Vs. Retention Costs – Statistics And Trends," invesp, November 11, 2020, https://www.invespcro.com/blog/customer-acquisition-retention/.

3   Customer Onboarding Statistics 2020," Wyzowl, accessed March 11, 2021, https://www.wyzowl.com/customer-onboarding-statistics/#:~:text=Over%2090%25%20of%20customers%20feel,them%20after%20they've%20bought.

- Fifty-five percent of people say they've returned a product because they didn't understand how to use it.[4]

- Highly engaged customers buy 90 percent more frequently, spend 60 percent more per transaction, and have three times the annual value of other customers.[5]

- Over 90 percent of customers think that companies "could do better" when it comes to onboarding new customers.[6]

Onboarding provides the bridge between the old sales Funnel and the new half of the Loop we're calling Client Expansion. Onboarding is the greatest opportunity to start building thriving relationships with our customers. It is a step the Funnel omits entirely, however, and thus it is a step that many companies miss or get wrong.

Onboarding: A Vital Step

What is onboarding? As its name suggests, it is the process of bringing customers "on board" after the purchase is complete. In "Funnel thinking," the purchase process ends with the sale. But for the customer, their *main experience with who we are* as a company (not as a sales unit) *begins* with the purchase.

From the customer's point of view, the marriage doesn't end at the wedding, it begins there. They've spent months "dating" us. They've selected us from among other suitors. They've signed the marriage contract and have accepted the risk that goes with that.

---

4   Ibid.

5   "80 Customer Service Statistics: 8 Lessons to Fuel Growth in 2020 and Beyond," Groove, accessed March 11, 2011, https://www.groovehq.com/customer-service-statistics.

6   "Customer Onboarding Statistics 2020," Wyzowl.

They're no longer a prospect, they're on board with us. And they can't wait to get started.

They have expectations and questions. *When do we kick off? When is my product shipping? Will I have a project manager? What's the next step?* They may have doubts and insecurities as well. *Did I do the right thing in signing with this company? Will this be good for my career?*

These doubts and questions only multiply the longer they go unaddressed. And yet, quite often, nothing happens after the contract signing. Crickets. This gap of inactivity can last anywhere from a couple of days to several weeks. Why? Maybe the company was so busy closing the order they haven't handed it over to the service team yet, and so the service team doesn't even know the customer exists yet. Maybe no one has been assigned to bridge the gap.

Or maybe the company *does* bridge the gap, but they do it in a clumsy, formulaic way that does not show respect and appreciation for the customer.

Bad Onboarding

Have you ever had an experience like this? You book a nice hotel for a few days away with your special someone. The hotel website wowed you with promised services and amenities, and you're really looking forward to the stay. You enter the lobby—your first encounter with the facility itself—and no one's at the front desk. You look around, you wait a minute or two. Nothing. You ring the bell for service, and no one comes. Growing impatient after five minutes, you check behind the counter or you peek into a back office to see if anybody's there—and suddenly someone barks at you, "You can't be back here!" You explain that you've been trying to check in, and they say, "Go back out to the lobby, I'll be with you in a minute."

Already you feel like an outsider, like you've done something wrong.

You go up to your room, and you find your keycard doesn't work, so you go back down to the desk, and you have to wait in line behind two other guests who are checking in. Fifteen minutes later you're finally able to get into your room, and it's not the room you reserved. You paid for an ocean view. So you call down, and the desk people react as if you've just dumped a problem on *them* and you should be grateful if they manage to solve it.

You're now feeling downright adversarial toward the place. You finally settle into your non-ocean-view room. You've just fallen asleep; it's 10:30 at night. The phone rings, and it's, *Good evening, sir. Just want to make sure you're enjoying your stay. Is there anything else we can do for you? Would you like a wake-up call? Don't forget to give us a reference on Instagram.*

Or maybe a B2B company has been wooing you, calling you every day at your office. You feel like you're getting to know the salesperson. When you chat together, you talk about sports and your kids and your interests. Then you sign the contract, and you're ready to be assigned a project manager. But the first thing you get is the bill. Suddenly you feel like all that personal chat was just phony. You feel used. You knew you were going to have to pay for what you bought, but you were hoping to be welcomed first—maybe some service?

Or perhaps you've made a service purchase and are waiting to find out what happens next. And nothing does. And nothing does. You eventually call the company, and they tell you, "We sent you an email explaining everything. Have you checked your junk folder?" Your attitude is, *Well hey, I'm on the phone with you right now, maybe* you *help me get started.* But no, they just want to point you back to that email you can't find.

All of these are examples of missed opportunities on the part of companies to do some great onboarding. What too few companies realize is that all of the customer's goals, hopes, and desires for the purchase first begin to be realized (or not) in the onboarding step. So when this step is skipped or handled clumsily, you have a disillusioned customer on your hands right from the get-go. All because the company is still viewing the customer as a *transaction*.

What the customer wants is a *relationship*. And if you ever want to turn that customer into a client, you need to invest in that relationship.

It's All About Emotion

There are a million practical, technical, and business reasons that a good onboarding process makes sense, but no reason is more important than emotion. As noted before, customers make purchases, even large ones—*especially* large ones—based on emotion first, logic second. And their emotions are very much in play after a significant purchase.

Customers are often feeling a wide range of emotions, including:

- I want to feel happy with this purchase.

- Did I make the right decision? Was I an idiot?

- Did I pay too much? Is this product/service worth what I paid?

- What am I supposed to do now?

- I'm excited to get started. I don't want to wait a day or a week or a month.

- The company pursued me endlessly before the purchase; are they going to abandon me now?

- What comes next? I'm feeling anxious and a little confused about upcoming steps.

- Am I going to be able to implement this product/service in my home/company?

- Will I get help trying to install or initialize it? What if something goes wrong? Whom do I call?

- Will my company get value from this product/service, or did I waste our money?

- I want to feel smart, like I made the best decision in the world.

- I want to look good to my team members.

- Will this purchase make my life easier or harder?

These are the kinds of emotions we should be anticipating and addressing in our onboarding. And here's a critical point: there should be *little to no gap* between the purchase and the beginning of onboarding. For example, my wife and I recently bought cars for two of our kids. As soon as the purchase was complete, the salesperson spent a half hour with each of them, showing them all the controls and features of the vehicles, driving around the lot with them, answering their questions. He then gave them a schedule of when to expect follow-up calls. They were brought into the "family" before they could leave the premises.

When there is a gap between the purchase and the next contact from the company, the customer begins to fill in that gap with anxieties, second thoughts, doubts, and stories. We don't want customers writing stories in their heads—*we* want to be the "storytellers" who craft a great experience.

Strategy Is Critical

It should be obvious by this point that a good onboarding process— one that amplifies the customer's positive emotions and lessens their negative emotions and anxieties—is essential. But unless we plan our onboarding strategically, we're likely going to have suboptimal results. A well-planned onboarding process can accomplish so much more than a scattershot approach.

Let's look at some essential strategies for planning our onboarding process ...

CREATE GOAL AND PLAN
1. Get users to use your product or service more than once within the first week
2. Establish a pattern of usage
3. Make your product indispensable

FUNDAMENTALS
1. Understand customers' expectations
2. Establish parameters
3. Competitor analysis
4. Key milestones

RESOURCES
1. Technology
2. Content

ESTABLISH KPIs
1. Specific
2. Measureable
3. Achieveable
4. Relevant
5. Time-bound

CREATE A GOAL AND PLAN

Right out of the gate we want to establish a pattern of how the customer is going to use our product or service. The more they use it,

> **Part of onboarding is to build up the use cases and address why the customer bought the product in the first place.**

the better. If the customer uses their purchase only sporadically, they're never going to get maximum value out of it. So part of onboarding is to build up the use cases and address why the customer bought the product in the first place. We want to make sure they're going to use the product/service consistently.

Toward that end, we want to get them to use it multiple times within a short period of time after the sale, if possible.

The goal is to make our product or service indispensable so that the customer can never imagine living without it again. Bottom line: create a plan that ensures the customer is regularly using the product/service toward the business goal they had in mind when they bought it. When our product or service becomes indispensable, we've taken the first concrete steps toward converting the customer to a client.

UNDERSTAND THE FUNDAMENTALS

We'll never be able to address the gaps in our onboarding unless we take the time to understand what the customer's expectations are. So we must talk to them, find out exactly what they're expecting from our product or service, and then do everything in our power, within reason, to meet or exceed their expectations. With that in mind, we set parameters for our onboarding program—exactly what we're going to do and not going to do.

When setting these parameters, it is helpful to know what our competitors are up to. If our five top competitors are rolling out the red carpet for their customers and we're just handing out bags of stale peanuts, we're probably falling short. Based on the parameters we decide on, we then establish some concrete milestones for the onboarding phase—specific actions we'll take, and dates by which they need to occur.

CLARIFY AND MOBILIZE RESOURCES

It's critical to understanding what resources we have available to us because sometimes onboarding is not a clearly "owned" function. Often there's a sales department and a service department, but no one's sure who is supposed to do the onboarding. That's why it is essential to do a RACI analysis: Who is Responsible for making sure the customer is onboarded properly? Who is Accountable? Whom do we Consult, and whom do we Inform?

Also, what tools, systems, platforms, and technologies are we going to use to facilitate a streamlined onboarding process? And what content do we need to develop and share with the customer that will be of highest value to them?

ESTABLISH KPIS

Finally: what isn't measured can't be managed. So we need to establish and track key performance indicators to tell us whether or not our onboarding process is working. These indicators should follow the SMART protocol—they should be Specific, Measurable, Achievable, Relevant, and Time-Bound. We might want to look, for example, at our customer churn and retention rates, our customers' time to adoption of our products and services, their content engagement levels, etc.

The Onboarding Process

There's no single onboarding process that makes sense for every company and customer type, but there are certain helpful steps we can do in most cases. All of these steps are simply ways to ensure that we're moving past the bell-ringing stage (the sale) and addressing the reality that the customer has needs that go beyond signing the contract. The steps don't necessarily occur in the following order.

1. Welcome Communication
2. Personalized Message
3. Product / Service Setup
4. Bridge Gaps
5. Highlight Product / Service Capabilities
6. Personalized Interaction
7. Establish Knowledge Base
8. Consistent Check-in
9. Celebrate Milestones

1. WELCOME COMMUNICATION

The very first thing we want to do is give the customer/client a feeling of being welcomed and appreciated. This can come in the form of a gift, a card, an email, a call—anything that says, "Hey, thanks so much for putting your trust in us. We appreciate you joining our 'family,' and we really hope you enjoy our product or service." This message needs to come *before* the invoice!

2. PERSONALIZED MESSAGE

Beyond the initial welcome—which might feel formulaic in some ways—there should be some sort of personalized touchpoint by which we check back with the customer a few days after the purchase and say something like, "Hey, Jim, just checking in. How's the [x] working out for you? Let me know if there's anything I can do." The more personal and specific we can make this communication, the better.

3. PRODUCT/SERVICE SETUP

Here's where we hold the customer's hand, tell them what to expect next, and guide them through whatever steps are necessary to get the product/service up and running. This may involve installation or configuration. Some installs take five minutes, some can take five months. If it's the latter, we have work to do. We can't just wait in silence for the setup to be completed. We need to communicate with the client—maybe through weekly status reports or via a landing page or app that displays milestones; maybe through a weekly call with our services team or project manager. We need to remember that the client may have eight other priorities they're working on. *We* need to be the ones who drive and focus this process.

4. BRIDGE THE GAPS

At some point—not at the very beginning, but not far down the road—we need to start understanding the gaps between what the customer was expecting from our company and what they feel they're getting. The way to do that is to *ask* them and also to observe what they're doing and not doing with the product. Once we understand what the gaps are, our job is to close those gaps. This may not always be fully possible—the customer might have some misunderstandings or some unrealistic expectations. In that case, all we can do is express that we're sorry and offer them some options. Otherwise we should try to solve their problem right on the spot or give them a plan for how their issues will be addressed.

5. HIGHLIGHT PRODUCT/SERVICE CAPABILITIES

Once the customer is steadily using the product, we want to make sure they're getting full utility from it. With lower-end items, it doesn't really matter if the customer is using only 20 percent of the functionality—after all, they only spent a hundred bucks—but if a client spends $10,000 or $250,000 for software, we want to make sure they're using it maximally. We can set up instructional calls, perhaps, or send weekly videos that explain a new feature each week. The more fully the client is using the product, the more indispensable it will become to them.

6. PERSONALIZED INTERACTIONS

Whenever we communicate with the customer after the purchase, we want to make our communications personal. This signals that we're invested in the relationship. One of the easiest ways to keep things personal is to use the customer's name and get it right—none of this "Dear Valued Customer" stuff. Even better is to remember something particular about the customer. We can say something like, "How is your daughter doing? Is she still enjoying her art program? I'd love to see some of her work."

7. ESTABLISH A KNOWLEDGE BASE

An important step in making sure onboarding is helpful and personal is to build a knowledge base of information and FAQ based upon multiple client interactions with the product as well as *this particular client's* interactions with the product and with us. An example of this is a hair salon where they let you check in online, they greet you by name when you walk in, they keep detailed notes about how you like your hair ("Do you still want the high bangs and the sweep on the side, Mary?"), and they know the products you buy and when they need to be refilled. The technology now exists to maintain highly personal profiles on each client—and to have that information readily available—yet few companies use this technology effectively.

8. CONSISTENT CHECK-IN

We never want to leave the customer feeling abandoned or forgotten during the onboarding process, so regular check-ins are vital. The longer the time horizon for the onboarding, the more regular the check-ins. These could be daily, weekly, or semimonthly, depending on the situation. As time goes on, we can use these check-ins to remind the customer of things they might miss on their own: benefits they may not have used yet, maintenance steps that need to be taken, warranty considerations. Of course, we don't want to badger the client either. We don't want to be like a waiter in a restaurant who asks you every two minutes if everything is okay—to which you want to reply, "It *would* be if you'd stop asking me if everything is okay."

9. CELEBRATE MILESTONES

Finally, it's a great idea to celebrate wins with our clients. "Hey, congratulations, Dan, I see you were able to launch your first campaign using our software," or "I see you just turned on [x level] of functionality, so that means your team training is right on schedule." Marking milestones with our clients shows we're paying attention to what they're actually using the product or service for, which builds trust and alignment.

Again, these steps will vary in importance and necessity with each type of product and customer, but they provide a good checklist for ensuring our onboarding is thorough and robust.

Now let's look at the next crucial stage in Client Expansion: adoption.

CHAPTER 7

ADOPTION

T he adoption stage takes us deeper into the Client Expansion side of the Loop. Here's where we take a further departure from Funnel thinking. The Funnel encourages us to think of Customer Acquisition in a transactional way. Our whole focus is on getting new customers to buy our products or existing customers to buy them again. We're not really paying attention to *how* our product or service is being used, only *that* it is being bought.

But if the customer is using only a portion of the product or service they bought, how will we ever be able to meet or exceed the expectations they had when they were considering buying in the first place? And if the customer's expectations aren't being met, why would they buy from us again or renew an existing purchase?

What this boils down to is: the degree to which the customer is *actually using the product* is critically important. They should be using the product *often*, they should be using the product *fully*, and they should be using the product *widely* (i.e., most of their team members, not merely a handful, should be using it).

We want the customer to get full value from our product or service so they feel good about the investment they made and are getting good ROI. That means they must *adopt* it and make it an integral part of their lives or businesses.

Size Matters

If a purchase is small and the customer uses only a fraction of it, that's not a big deal. If I buy a six-pack of granola bars and I eat only three of them, no one's going to lose any sleep. But if a customer pays a hundred thousand dollars for a piece of office equipment and it lies dormant or underutilized, that's a problem. That means the customer is getting little to no ROI. Why would they even begin to want to buy from us again?

Take a country club, for example. Not cheap to join. If I purchase a membership, I probably do it for several reasons. I want to play golf. I want to socialize. I want to have some good meals. I want a sense of community. But in practice, it might turn out that I'm only playing golf. I'm not doing the social stuff, I'm not taking advantage of the spa or the free babysitting, I'm not using the pro shop or the restaurant. At the end of the year, I may look back and realize the family only went to the club together twice. And so when I look at my annual dues, I will very likely say, "Why on earth am I paying $30,000 a year for *this*?"

The same thing can happen on a business level. A customer buys our software, and it has a hundred great features. But the customer is using only five of them. Or the customer has bought licenses for a hundred users, but only ten of them are logging in every day; the other ninety haven't logged in in six months. That's poor ROI, and that's a problem.

Usage Is Critical

We want to maximize usage of our product or service. Onboarding was about helping the customer make the bridge from purchaser to user. Adoption is a deeper form of onboarding. It's about carrying the customer past the honeymoon period and into full immersion with the product/service.

We want the customer to improve their business, get a good ROI, gain ease and enjoyment, and achieve the outcomes they wanted to achieve. That happens only when they're using our products and services as fully as possible and reaping all of our products' benefits. That is why smart businesses work so hard to drive adoption.

Have you ever wondered, for example, why companies work so hard to push "free" services or services you've already paid for on you? Maybe that country club, for example, sends out constant invites to its free cocktail hour on Thursdays. Or maybe your home warranty company pushes you to avail yourself of its free annual air-conditioning tune-up. You might say, "This stuff is included in the membership fee I've already paid. It's going to cost the company money to provide it. Aren't they better off financially if I pay for it but don't use it?"

No. Your country club *wants* you to come in and consume "free" drinks and snacks every Thursday because it wants you to adopt the club as an integral part of your lifestyle—so you'll renew your membership next year. The home warranty company *wants* you to arrange the free tune-up because that will force you to go through its online process of scheduling a home service visit, thereby making you an actual user of their system.

> **Adoption is about turning customers into satisfied regular users who don't want to live without our products. In turn, those customers become clients.**

Adoption is about turning customers into satisfied regular users who don't want to live without our products. In turn, those customers become clients.

Strategies for Driving Adoption

As with onboarding, a scattershot approach to getting customers to adopt our products will produce scattershot results. We need to design a thoughtful adoption process, and for that, we need a strategy. Here are the core elements of adoption strategy that we teach to our TPG clients:

1 BLUEPRINT
- Ideal customer adoption journey
- Requirements
- Touchpoints
- Goals

2 PLAN
- Outcomes
- Milestones
- Content

3 MEASURE
- Data
- Value
- KPIs

4 SEGMENT
- Product / Service
- Health
- Attributes

5 ENGAGE
- Content
- Training
- Relationships

1. BLUEPRINT

First, we try to determine the ideal adoption journey for our various customers so that they can enjoy full usage of our products and services. And then we design that experience for each customer. Adoption is a very different journey from purchasing. Let's take a college student, for example. Getting them to select our school, apply, and enroll is the *purchase journey*. By contrast, getting them to matriculate, take their classes, and become an active participating member of the student body is the *adoption journey*. Toward that end, certain requirements must be met—they must finish the first semester with passing grades, pay their tuition, finish the second semester, etc. To help them accomplish this and to encourage full adoption, we provide service touchstones—we assign the student an academic advisor, we arrange meet and greets with professors, we provide learning labs and social events. We design numerous interactions so the student can have an immersive experience. Our goal is for the student to earn their degree with us, but also, ideally, to become a successful alumnus who will give back to the school and attract more students in the future.

2. PLAN

Based on our blueprint, we plan our execution. What content will we need? What resources? Who will be RACI (Responsible, Accountable, Consulted, Informed)? What key milestones must be reached along the way, and what outcomes do we want? Outcomes are different from goals. Our *goal* might be to achieve 90 percent adoption of our product or for our average customer to buy three products. But examples of *outcomes* are: the client is able to increase their product efficiency by 17 percent, their revenue by 30 percent, and their market share by 15 percent—as a result of using our product.

3. MEASURE

If we really care about our client, we won't just focus on their renewal date—we'll look at whether or not they're getting real business value and outcomes from our product or service. How will we know this unless we measure—and measure the things that matter? What kind of data do we need in order to understand the business value they're getting? We must establish some KPIs that are meaningful and measurable (SMART). We might want to look, for example, at user satisfaction rates, at the percentage of objectives that are being attained in business cases, or at the rate of successful changes being implemented through use of the product.

4. SEGMENT

No two customers are the same. While there will always be overlap between use cases, the way one customer in one industry uses our product may be completely different from the way another does. So there's no one-size-fits-all adoption strategy. Depending on who our customers are and what their needs are, we might need to design different adoption paths for each type of customer.

We should look at things like the "health" of the client (are they thriving or struggling?), as well as their psychographic, behavioral, and demographic attributes. And then we need to segment them into categories so we can address their adoption needs in a customized way.

5. ENGAGE

Finally, of course, we need to engage. We must create an ongoing conversation. Marriage doesn't work if the two partners don't talk to each other. We must actively collaborate with the customer in order to create meaningful content that drives their goals. We must commit to ongoing training—training with the client on how to better use our product/service and training within our own team on how to better drive client adoption—as well as great service and support. We do all of this with the specific intent of building relationships. After all, the client is not just adopting our products and services, the client is adopting *us*.

Adoption Principles

There are a few helpful principles to keep in mind when creating adoption programs for and with customers. Remember to:

Help with Change Management—The whole point of selling a product or service is to disrupt, to innovate, and/or to help our clients do something they couldn't do before. So if we're really trying to get the client to adopt our products/services, we can't just think about the features our product offers, we must think about how we can help the client *manage the change* in their organization that goes along with using our product or service.

Synchronize Old and New—We need to help the client bridge the gap between what they were doing before and what they're able to do now that they're using our product or service. Most companies can't just throw out everything they were doing before and immediately start doing something new. We need to understand where clients are coming *from* in order to help them get where they're going *to*.

Provide Training and Education—Training and education must be ongoing, not just a one-shot thing. And we must be patient and understanding with our "students."

Demonstrate Value and Purpose—It's on us to continually demonstrate that the client is getting value and purpose from our product/

service and from their interactions with us. We need to do this in as many different ways and from as many different angles as we can.

Achieve Executive and Stakeholder Alignment—If the executives at the client company don't support the product/service we're selling, we might get a sale, sure, but it won't be one that leads to a long-term relationship. So we must commit to building alignment between the executives and the stakeholders so that the whole company adopts whatever we're selling.

Develop Influential Champions—It's always wise to cultivate one or more "evangelists" for our business within the client company, people who will recommend us every chance they get. These people should ideally be influencers who have credibility and the respect of their peers. Influencers are crucial because they will help us create the next product wave.

Do Scaled Implementation—Very few companies do massive rollouts from initial contracts anymore. People want to manage their risk. So when driving adoption of our product or service, we want to think about proceeding in metered ways that deliver incremental, pragmatic wins.

Monitor Adoption and Usage—If the only thing we're monitoring and measuring is when the contract renews, we're not going to have very good renewal rates or strong Adoption. We need to devise ways to measure those three variables I mentioned early in the chapter: how *often*, how *fully*, and how *widely* the client is using our product/service.

If we do all of this, we can create muscular adoption programs that lead to an even more important step in Client Expansion: Value Realization.

CHAPTER 8

VALUE REALIZATION

alue realization is a vital step in turning users into loyal fans and advocates. In my experience, a lot of companies don't really understand what value realization is and why it is important. Sometimes we confuse it with onboarding and adoption. We assume our job is done once we've gotten the customer up and running with our product/service.

We are often so focused on the *transaction*, on getting the customer to buy more, that we're asking the customer the wrong questions after the sale. We're asking questions like, *Are you happy with the product? Would you recommend our product to a friend or a business associate? On a scale of one to ten, how would you rate our service?*

Such questions don't help us ascertain whether or not the product or service is actually *helping the customer do the things the customer bought it for.*

No matter how well adopted a product or service is, if it's not creating real value for the customer—as the *customer* defines value—then it's not a net gain for them. Our product might be technologically impressive, it might be prestigious, it might be fun to use, but if it is not producing specific value, it will soon be forgotten. The customer will move on.

Companies often miss the mark on value realization, but it is essential. After all, how can you expect to move forward with a client if they are not getting maximal value from the stuff you've already sold them? How can you expect to build a lasting and loyal relationship?

Again, if we're talking about a small, onetime purchase, no one loses sleep if it fails to produce full value. But the costlier the product/service is and the more potential it has to lead to repeat business, the more important value realization becomes.

Customers Want Outcomes

It goes without saying that if someone buys a product or service, they want to use it. If you buy a car, you want to drive it. If you buy a television, you want to watch it. A product needs to live up to its basic functionality promises. But that is only the beginning of its value maximization. A customer doesn't pay for a product just to get *usage* out of it; the product must help them do something they couldn't do before or help them do it *in a better way* than they could before.

We need to know the outcome our customer is trying to achieve—whether consciously or unconsciously—by buying our product or service. We also need to know the outcome the customer *could* achieve if they fully adopted the product and understood its features. And we need to make an ongoing effort to ensure these optimal outcomes are being achieved.

Value realization can play out a bit differently in B2C (business-to-customer) and B2B situations, but the underlying principles remain the same.

VALUE REALIZATION IN THE B2C WORLD

Consumers spend money on products, services, and experiences for any number of reasons. Sometimes they know exactly the value they are trying to achieve—"I'm buying this hot air balloon flight because I want to surprise my mate with an exciting and romantic adventure"—and sometimes they don't. They may buy a product because it has cool features, because they are curious about it, because it was marketed cleverly, or a hundred other reasons, but they may not fully realize the value it *could* bring them.

Let's take an "Alexa" product or similar voice-activated device. A customer may buy it or receive it as a gift with the vague promise that it will improve their life but may end up using it only as a music player they listen to while cooking meals. Low-level value. But what if the customer knew, for example, they could use the device to verbally ...

- set timers for cooking,

- order products from Amazon and check order statuses,

- set helpful reminders throughout the day—to drink water at planned intervals, to take medication, to pick up their kid at school, to defrost a roast,

- program the thermostat,

- check on the status of a flight,

- check the weather—or weather forecast—in any city or town in the world,

- record Sunday's football game on TV,

- listen to a book or TED talk,

- find out encyclopedia-type facts on millions of topics,

- learn new recipes,

… and so on? If the customer began to realize the true value of a device like this—i.e., *it makes my life more manageable, efficient, and mistake free*—then that customer might buy a similar device for the upstairs or the vacation home, give the device to a friend as a gift, and rave about the device to family and friends. The customer might also invest in other home devices that were "Alexa"-compatible—garage door openers, TVs, thermostats, ovens, etc. When *value* is realized, the device becomes integral to the customer's life.

> **When *value* is realized, the device becomes integral to the customer's life.**

Often we sell (or fail to sell) items to customers without knowing the true value we're selling. For example, my family has a tradition that every year at Christmas we dress in holiday pajamas— new ones every year—and take a family photo. For several years, I've been buying these PJs from a specialty pajama retailer, but I've begun to cool in my loyalty of late. Part of this cooling is because the family is getting older, so they're not as "into it" as they used to be, but it's also because the product is expensive. I might not mind spending $65 for a set of pajamas for my wife, but it's a steep price to pay when buying five sets that are only going to be worn once or twice.

It strikes me that the seller may not understand the value I'm shopping for. Sure, every year they send me mailings about Christmas pajamas, but they're looking at it from a "how many sets of PJs can we sell this year?" point of view. What *I'm* really buying is *memories*, not pajamas. If they understood they were in the business of selling memories, they might, for example, offer me suggestions for taking more creative holiday photos (or an app for doing this), offer to sell me a nice scrapbook for my past Christmas memories, or include the family pets in the product sales. I'd be happy to spend a few hundred dollars for memories. For pajamas? Not so much.

Or think, for example, of the experience of taking your family to a ball game. Between the tickets, the parking, the food, and the merchandise, the cost rivals a mortgage payment. What are you paying for? Not for a better view of the game—you can see the action just as well, or better, on TV. You're paying for an *exciting live-entertainment experience.* Anything the seller can do to create an enhanced sensory experience will help realize this value. On the other hand, if there's a drunk guy behind you yelling obscenities, the food is cold, the bathroom is filthy, and the souvenir shop has run out of your favorite jersey, you will probably conclude you did not receive value for your investment.

A company must always strive to ensure that the highest value of its products and services is being realized.

VALUE REALIZATION IN THE B2B WORLD

When it comes to B2B, it is essential for us to understand that businesses buy our products and services to achieve *business outcomes.* We're not selling them vanity or prestige or vague concepts like "authority," "market leadership," or "visibility." Sure, we may use terms like those in our marketing campaigns, but what we're really delivering are outcomes. A business client that buys our products and services is ultimately thinking only one thing: "I paid x amount of money for this, I'd better get a concrete business outcome that's worth the investment."

Examples of business outcomes are:

- increased revenue

- better process efficiency

- improved throughput

- reduced costs

- higher productivity

- fewer customer complaints

- reduced waste

- saving of time

- fewer product returns

- improved product reviews

The types of things they talk about in boardrooms.

Abstract values—such as happier employees and cooler branding—are important to achieve too, but if we're not contributing to business outcomes, the customer will move on.

We're Asking the Wrong Questions

To achieve value realization, we must ask the right questions of our customers, both before and after the sale. This means, once again, we can't be narcissistic. We can't be thinking about moving customers down *our* Funnel so we can ring *our* bell and accomplish *our* business outcome—a sale. We must be exploring the *customer's* needs and trying to find ways to help them achieve *their* outcome. Again, this means developing a *relationship* with the client so that we can truly understand their unique requirements and circumstances.

BEFORE THE SALE

The better we can understand during the Client Acquisition phase the specific outcomes customers are looking for, the better we can tailor our products and services toward addressing those outcomes—and the earlier we can set up intelligent KPIs for tracking our success. During Client Acquisition, we also need to help the customer understand the *additional* value we can bring to their business, beyond what they may be specifically looking for.

AFTER THE SALE

During Client Expansion, we need to ensure that value is being realized for the customer. The way most B2C companies—and many B2B ones as well—do this is through satisfaction surveys. This is a weak and impersonal approach, even when done well, but many companies do it poorly. Instead of asking meaningful, targeted, and data-based questions, they ask vague and subjective ones such as: *Are you happy with the product? Would you refer us to a friend?*

Such questions are based on emotion. So if this morning, for example, I asked you if you were happy with my product, you might be in a good mood—you got your workout in, you just received a nice email from a friend—so you might give me four and a half stars. Another day I might ask you the same question, and maybe your furnace just broke, you got an unexpected bill in the mail … On that day you'll give me two and a half stars.

Emotion-based answers don't help us improve our products and services to deliver more value to customers. Objective questions with quantifiable answers are better. What we should be asking customers is: *Has my product or service helped you save time? Has it helped you make more money? Save money? Has it netted you more sales? Has it reduced your product returns?*

And whenever possible we should ask such questions directly—in person or on the phone—rather than in multiple-choice questionnaires. The first thing we should try to determine is the business need for which the client bought the product. Then we should tailor our questions to assessing whether or not that need is being met. And if the need is not being fully met, we must come up with a plan for making changes.

To do this requires having a real relationship with real people.

Value Realization Strategy

To help clients/customers achieve full value realization, again we must have a disciplined, strategic approach, not a random or sporadic one. The steps of a good value realization strategy usually include:

PLAN CAPABILITIES
- What capabilities will your product / service help your customer achieve?
- What combination of people, process, technology, and skill at your client's organizational level?

VALUE MANAGEMENT
- Systems
- Processes
- KPIs

OPERATIONAL MODEL AND GOVERNANCE
- Standards
- Benchmarking
- Controls
- Procedures

RESOURCE MANAGEMENT
- Client Resource Identification
- Client Stakeholder Alignment
- Client Executive Sponsorship

CUSTOMER MANAGEMENT
- Customer Success Managers
- Success Management Plan
- KPI Monitoring

DECISION SUPPORT
- Business Intelligence
- Data Visualization
- Predictive Modeling

1. PLAN CAPABILITIES

Planning our capabilities begins with asking, "What does our product or service do?" and "What capabilities will it help the customer achieve?" It's not so much about showing off the features on our widget, it's about helping the customer do what they couldn't do *without* our widget. It's about thoroughly understanding the capabilities our client can get from our product or service and how those capabilities will be achieved—i.e., what combination of people, process, technology, and skill will we need to deploy at an organizational level?

2. VALUE MANAGEMENT

Next we need to figure out how to measure, on a proactive basis, whether our client is getting the value they want from us. What systems, processes, technologies, and KPIs are we going to track and measure—as opposed to just asking the client, "Are you happy with us?" Toward that end, we need to look at what features and functions of our products they're employing. But that still might not tell us whether they're actually making money, improving productivity, etc.

Let's say, for example, we manufacture medical equipment used in surgery. What we need to look at is not just the utility of our product—we addressed that in Onboarding and Adoption—but the value it is giving the organization. We might measure things like patient survival rates, average length of surgery times, and recovery times of patients. We might count the number of physicians using the equipment and the number of additional OR (operating room) blocks that open up as a result of using our equipment. These things translate into concrete business value.

3. OPERATIONAL MODEL AND GOVERNANCE

Next we start setting standards and benchmarks. Staying with the medical equipment example, let's say we've installed our equipment at five hundred hospitals, and they've reduced their surgical time by 30 percent on average and their patient recovery times by 25 percent. Those become our standards. Benchmarks are the numbers we *derive* from the standards: When compared to other businesses using the same standards, is our client's number higher or lower than the benchmark? That starts to tell us whether or not the client is headed for getting value or not.

Let's say our client is only reducing patient recovery time by 10 percent. That's not good enough. What is in our control, and what are we going to do about it? Did we do something wrong in the training? Is the equipment defective? Do we need to do some observation? What procedures will we put in place to make sure the client is getting back on course?

4. RESOURCE MANAGEMENT

Once we establish that people in the client company are using and getting value from the product, we need to proactively identify and work with these users—not just with the person who signed the contract and pays the invoices. Who are the people *actually using* our product or service? In the previous example, these might be the surgeons and technicians. How do we begin to have a relationship with them?

How, too, do we make sure that all the stakeholders—the chief of surgery and the hospital administrator, for example—have an aligned and supportive point of view toward our product or service? And how do we gain *sponsorship* for our product within the executive team (e.g., the hospital administrator)?

It does no good, ultimately, to have users and stakeholders raving about our product if the fiscal decision-maker does not perceive its value. The hospital administrator, for instance, might be facing a scenario where total hospital revenue is down by 10 percent. She might appreciate our product's utility, but she might say, "It costs a half million dollars. We can't afford it." It's on us to show her that use of the product will result in an increase in the number of surgeries and a reduction in operating costs, etc., such that the half million invested now will generate five times that revenue over the next six months. Now we're talking her language. Now we're solving her business problem. Now she may become our *sponsor*.

5. CUSTOMER MANAGEMENT

Next, we need to invest in watching and working with the customer on an ongoing basis. Many companies today work with customers on a subscription basis, and they've discovered that simply *subscribing* customers is not enough. To ensure a low churn rate every year, they now assign a customer success manager. This person, typically not a high-level resource, is tasked with checking in with customers on a regular basis to make sure they're getting what they need. This provides a human touch, and many companies have found it ends up saving them millions of dollars each year. Building a success management plan means determining what the success criteria will look like for the customer and then monitoring these KPIs every day.

6. DECISION SUPPORT

Finally, at an executive level within our own company, we need to take a top-down look at all our customers and ask questions like: *How much value does each customer represent? Are any customers beginning to slip away? Which customers are more likely to renew? Where do we have potential problems? Potential opportunities?*

Here's where we also look at developing tools to help us—things like data visualization and predictive modeling. Are we able to visualize and understand the data we're getting from customers? Is the customer able to visualize the data that helps them make decisions about using our products? Can we develop some good predictive modeling that will help current and potential clients understand the savings and revenue they can realize by using our products? In short, can we develop better tools for demonstrating and maximizing our value to customers?

***

Remember: just because we've got a great brand or ultracool marketing doesn't mean we've made inroads with the customer. Ultimately, if our customers aren't getting real-life value or business value from our product or service, they're going to look to other options. If we do a great job with Value Realization, however, customer loyalty is almost certain to follow.

CHAPTER 9

LOYALTY

A s opposed to value realization, which many companies don't adequately consider, Loyalty is an area most companies are quite mindful of. In fact, marketers spend a lot of time, energy, and creativity designing loyalty programs—especially if they are in consumer businesses.

The airlines are a great example. Their mileage programs have been attracting loyal customer bases for years. Hotels that offer free stays for every several paid ones, credit cards that offer customer reward points, and stores that offer special discounts for "members only" are just a few examples of the ways companies encourage brand loyalty and repeat usage of their products or services.

For many B2B organizations, there just isn't the same kind of effort and consistency put into building loyalty. We all *want* loyalty from our clients, sure, but we don't always know what to do in order to build it.

It is certainly more challenging to create loyalty programs within a B2B environment—especially a high-end one. After all, if we're selling multimillion-dollar surgical robots to hospitals, we can't hand our customers punch-cards and say, "For every ten surgical robots you buy, you get one free!"

We'll talk about some of the B2B challenges in a minute, but first let's talk about loyalty itself and how we create it. The essentials of loyalty building are the same, whether we're in a B2C or a B2B situation.

What Is Loyalty, and How Do We Foster It?

In some ways, loyalty is a natural thing. We humans are creatures of habit. We are loyal to our friends and family. We are loyal to our political parties. We are loyal to the foods we eat, the places we visit, and the music we listen to.

We are even loyal to our brands. When we find something that works for us, we tend to repeat it over and over again.

If you live in the Northeast, for example, it's likely you're either a Starbucks person or a Dunkin' Donuts person. You have your loyalty—but, of course, it's not absolute, and it's subject to conditions. You might really like Dunkin' Donuts, but the nearest Dunk's might be ten miles from your hotel and there may be four Starbucks within two miles. Do you drive ten miles to get to Dunkin', or do you go to the Starbucks?

If you're really, really loyal to Dunkin' Donuts, you'll make the ten-mile trip. But hey, it's only coffee. So maybe you'll go to Starbucks today.

Habit-wise, we might change it up now and then, but more often than not we're going to buy our favored thing. Unless, of course, someone else can get our attention and give us a better experience. If you find yourself going to that Starbucks four days in a row, and you start to really appreciate their drive-through experience, you may become a Starbucks person before you know it. Or vice versa. Suddenly your loyalty has changed.

In many ways, that is the role of marketing: to make customers form new loyalties—in the face of intense competition from other players. How do we do that? What are the principles that drive loyalty, both in the B2C and B2B worlds? Here are a few …

1. DELIVER A GREAT CUSTOMER EXPERIENCE

The main way we win customers away from their present loyalties and start building loyalty with *us* is by delivering an excellent customer experience. We do that by delighting the customer, by making the buying process easier for them, by honoring and respecting them, and by appreciating their time constraints—by putting *them*, not ourselves, center stage.

Chick-fil-A, for example, has taken the drive-through experience to a whole new level in many locations. Staffers stand outside, waiting to greet you as you drive up. They take your order, and you pay from your car. They direct you into the best lane. It's all very efficient, and you feel taken care of throughout the process.

Starbucks created a cutting-edge app for smartphones that was way ahead of many other restaurants and retailers. It allows you to do much more than just buy your food. You can order ahead, buy merchandise, restock your card. They even added proximity tracking so they know when you're getting physically near the shop, and they know your preferences as well. It's a seamless customer experience that's easy and enjoyable.

2. CREATE CONSISTENCY

A major driver of brand loyalty is consistency. Can the customer count on your product and/or service to deliver the same dependable quality each time they purchase it? Can they count on the customer experience to be a predictable (and positive) one?

In many ways, consistency is even more important than excellence. A McDonald's hamburger might not be better than the handmade burger next door, but the customer knows exactly what they're getting every time. A cup of Dunkin' Donuts coffee might not offer a high-end gourmet experience, but it's good and reliable. Dunkin' works hard to ensure that a cup of its coffee tastes the same, no matter which of its twelve thousand locations you buy it at.

> **When excellence and consistency are combined, magic happens.**

When excellence and consistency are combined, magic happens. In-N-Out Burger has developed legions of rabid fans who will drive thirty miles out of their way for a burger. How have they done that? By delivering high quality *and* consistency.

3. TREAT CUSTOMERS WELL WHEN THINGS GO WRONG

Customer loyalty can actually take a quantum leap when things go *wrong*. Does the company abandon the customer with a "sorry, not my problem" attitude, or does it bend over backward to make things right for the customer? The response of the company to its own mistakes should be so positive that it more than makes up for the inconvenience of the original error.

For example, a restaurant that ruins a customer's meal should not only remove the bad meal from the bill, it should offer a personal apology, a free dessert, and perhaps even a voucher for a future meal.

An airline that bumps a customer from a flight should not only pay for a hotel room but also offer the customer free miles for the future. A mistake on the part of the company is actually an *opportunity* to create an even stronger bond with a customer.

4. SURPRISE THE CUSTOMER/CLIENT

Doing nice things for customers and clients randomly and unexpectedly is a great way to build loyalty. Send them a gift, give them an upgrade, buy them a free drink, do something thoughtful that goes above and beyond the contract. Few gestures are more loyalty-inspiring than the random act of kindness and appreciation. Also, contact the client at unexpected times, just to check in, say hello, see how they're doing.

5. ANTICIPATE NEEDS

Being so customer centric that we anticipate the client's needs and solve them proactively is loyalty gold. A great hotel, for example, thinks about what their individual guests might need given the time of their arrival, the purpose of their visit, the history of their preferences, etc. So if a guest arrives, for example, hours past their expected arrival time and late at night, the staff can assume they are tired and that their travel plans went awry. Going out to their car to greet them and help them with their bags, or giving them a complimentary nightcap or cup of herbal tea says, *We're taking care of you.*

6. ESTABLISH A BRAND WITH STRONG IDENTITY

A key to building lasting loyalty is to establish a strong brand that stands for identifiable values and then delivering on that brand's promises. Customers like to feel an affinity with the brands they support; they like to feel like they're members of a special club.

7. FINALLY, BUILD TRUST—THE
ULTIMATE LOYALTY PROGRAM

And, of course, we should strive to build trust. Trust develops slowly, through repeated encounters with our company, our brand. Do we deliver on all of these factors repeatedly and predictably? Do we put the client first in all of our encounters with them? Do we know who we are and who our customers are? If we can develop trust, loyalty will automatically follow.

Challenges in the B2B Environment

As noted earlier, it's a bit trickier in a B2B environment to do "loyalty programs" of the type we can do in a consumer environment, but if we keep the previous principles in mind, we can use them as the bedrock of our loyalty efforts.

There is an additional loyalty challenge in the B2B environment, which is that loyalty is not monolithic. By that, I mean there are different buying centers and individuals within the client company with whom we do business. Not all of them are loyal to us in the same way or to the same degree.

Essentially, that creates four potential scenarios when it comes to loyalty:

- The client company is loyal to us, but its people are not.

- The people are loyal, but the company is not.

- *Some* people within the company are loyal, others are not.

- Both the company *and* its people are loyal.

All of these scenarios, except the final one (to which we aspire), create challenges for us.

We might, for example, have a loyal ally within the company who has bought from us for years, but now their procurement department prefers another vendor. Or the client company might have a contract in place with us, but individuals throughout the company are subverting the contract because they don't like us. They're buying from their own people on the side.

So how do we address these various scenarios?

We start by having a strategy and a proactive plan. We don't take a Funnel approach, which is to simply return to the top of the Funnel and start on a new logo. Rather, we strategically focus on growing the logo we already have, complete with all of its challenges.

Loyalty Strategy

Whether we're in a fairly simple B2C situation or a layered and complex B2B world, being strategic and disciplined in our approach to loyalty building will put us on the path to success. Here is the strategy approach we use at TPG:

PROGRAM STRATEGY

To develop loyalty with our customers requires creating a plan. First we need to identify what our goals are. What are we trying to accomplish? Who are all the people with whom we are trying to build loyalty? If we're in a B2B situation, do we have multiple loyalty centers within the company that we need to address? What are the different approaches we'll need for each?

PROGRAM DESIGN

Now how are we going to design a loyalty program? What elements does it need to have? We must look at the seven loyalty principles and plan some specific ways to address them. How can we create a great customer experience? How will we treat clients when we screw up? What can we do for our clients that's thoughtful and unexpected?

Rewards are also an essential component of loyalty plans. We need to plan how we are going to reward our customers. In a B2C situation and some B2B situations, we can use a physical reward such as points, discounts, or gifts. If so, the reward needs to align with the value of our product/service. A free frozen yogurt won't cut it when you're selling million-dollar consulting services.

In other cases, the reward we give our client can come in the form of intangibles, such as stature or respect. We might, for example, invite the client onto our advisory board, include them in a book we're writing, or publish an interview with them. We might invite them to speak at a user conference, present at a board meeting, or join a product review group. No one way works for every person and every situation. We need to come up with a comprehensive approach and plan accordingly.

REWARDS STRATEGY AND FULFILLMENT

Essentially, we have to find out what our customers want and give it to them in a way they will value. We can give it to them via formal rewards but also in informal ways, tailoring our rewards to the audience we're trying to win. So if we're selling to surgeons, we might appeal to their intellect and their skill. This might involve providing them opportunities, not only to use our product but to weigh in on its future design.

We must try to think, *If I were buying my stuff, what would I want?* And we don't need to guess about this, we can ask our customers directly: "What would be a perfect customer experience for you, from the moment you start considering our product or service?" We'll get different answers, but if we talk to enough people, we'll get enough data points to shape our programs. Ask clients what they hate too—sometimes it's easier for them to remember *bad* experiences, such as having salespeople disrespect their schedules, than good ones.

MARKETING COMMUNICATION
STRATEGY AND PLANNING

Once we have our loyalty program planned, marketing plays an important role in communicating with the customer. The more elaborate our program, the greater the need for interactive websites and self-rating systems and the like, and the greater the importance of communicating our messages via multiple channels.

But there are many ways we can instill loyalty in much simpler ways too—such as sending a personalized birthday or Christmas card or a personalized gift. A handwritten note goes a long way. With larger customers, we can offer to take them out for a thank-you lunch or dinner. But, as with anything else, if we don't *plan* our communications strategically and make someone accountable for them, they won't happen.

PROGRAM ORGANIZATION AND PROCEDURES

Similarly, if we don't put a structure around our loyalty program, it just becomes a thing we *want* to do but eventually gets deprioritized and falls apart. If we really want to have an effective loyalty program, we need to run it as vigorously as we do the top of the Funnel.

TECHNOLOGY

Finally, where appropriate, we need to deploy the appropriate technology for our program. For many retail loyalty programs, that might mean creating a mobile app. In other businesses, we may not need that, but we might still need some form of tech to stay in touch with customers, send them rewards and surprises, gather their feedback, monitor their usage, and so on.

If we succeed in turning customers into loyal fans, we may be able to move them to that holy grail of Client Engagement: advocacy.

CHAPTER 10

ADVOCACY

L oyalty—consistent customers who make repeat purchases—is a great thing to achieve. Every company is thrilled to win the steady revenue that loyal customers provide.

But loyalty has its limits. It doesn't spread *exponentially*. It's not as if every loyal Starbucks customer is out there evangelizing about their coffee experience. No, most people go to Starbucks because when they use their app and buy x number of coffees, they get a freebee. They use their Delta credit card because they earn frequent flyer miles on Delta. They use their American Express card because they earn points.

In other words, they're loyal to a brand because they're getting a good customer experience and because repeat purchases bring them predictable benefits.

Loyalty is wonderful, but it requires constant efforts on the part of the company to get the customer/client to *do* something. Advocacy is different. When clients become advocates, they're out there promoting us on their own. They're not waiting for us.

A good example of this is when you have a great meal at a restaurant and you spontaneously tell all your friends, "Hey, we just had some fantastic barbecue, you have to try this place." Or if you read a great book or see a fabulous show on Netflix or HBO, and you tell everyone on social media about it. You want your friends to have the same great experience you had (and to show what great taste you have).

In a B2B context, advocacy usually occurs a bit more contextually. Perhaps, for example, you hear that a colleague is considering pursuing a certain type of consulting service, and you tell them, "You might want to try Firm A because we had a great experience with them." Again, no one asked you to do that, you just did it on your own—when the opportunity arose.

While loyalty is about our clients' *own* purchasing behavior, advocacy is about what they say to *others*. Not only is advocacy free advertising, it is also the highest form of endorsement our products and services can receive. When a happy user voluntarily raves about our products/services, that's pure gold.

A lot of companies—both on the B2C and B2B sides—understand loyalty but miss the mark when it comes to advocacy. That's because many of us tend to think that advocacy is something that, almost by definition, happens "on its own."

But advocacy is something we can and should plan for.

Degrees of Advocacy

By nature, people advocate for different types of products and services in different ways. For example, people love to evangelize about technology products for some reason. There's a certain sector of the population that loves to become early testers and adopters of new software programs and tech devices. They jump on the forums the day the product is announced and start talking about it to their peers and to the public.

We see this in B2B software; we also see it in consumer and entertainment software, such as computer games. The same thing happens with smartphones, tablets, and a whole host of other products where people like to try them first and then if they have a great experience tell the world. Look at Apple—it has had a veritable army of advocates for years. If we can get the right people loving our technology and using it early, they can become major advocates for us.

This doesn't occur so much with other types of services. For example, you don't necessarily brag about using a lawyer or a psychologist or a chemical-spill cleanup service. These services tend to be a bit more private and discretionary. But if you're in the right conversation at the right time with someone you trust, you might offer up a referral.

There are still other products and services that fall somewhere in the middle. You may be delighted with the service you received, but you might not be shouting it from the rafters.

Obviously, this means we need to differentiate our approach when it comes to seeking advocates. Every situation is different.

Advocacy Strategy

When developing an advocacy strategy, we need to think along two axes. First we need to think about the *who*. What type of person am I trying to groom as an advocate? Second we need to think about the *what*. What is our desired outcome? It helps to picture these axes visually. We adapted the following chart from one designed by the Center for Evaluation Innovation, a nonprofit agency that deals with public policy and philanthropy.

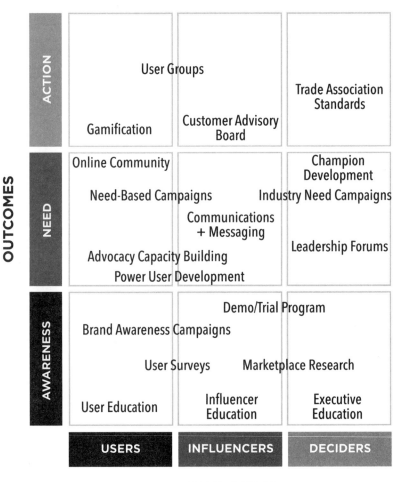

ADVOCATE TYPES

Generally speaking, we need to look at three different types of potential advocates within our client companies (see the *x* axis). Each will need a different approach from us. They are:

- **Users**—These are the people who are actually using our product on a regular basis. Let's take the medical equipment example again. In this case, our users would be the surgeons. Users can be great advocates because they know the product in a practical, intimate way and can influence their peers to use it.

- **Influencers**—These are respected users of the product/service or people on the management team whose opinion about the product can have a wide influence within the organization. These can also be people in social media or the press. In the medical example, an influencer might be the department chair or chief of surgery, or perhaps a nurse practitioner who is well respected within the surgical wing. Influencers have the capacity to ... well, *influence.*

- **Deciders**—These are the people who have the power to make the decision as to whether their company will actually buy our services or products. The hospital administrator is an example. Obviously, deciders are key advocates within the organization—without them, the product doesn't get purchased. But deciders can also be hugely influential within their greater industry and with peer organizations.

DESIRED OUTCOMES

As we're looking at who our advocates can be, we also need to look specifically at what we need or want our advocates to *do* for us (see the *y* axis in the previous graphic). Do we want them to …

- **Create awareness**—Are we simply trying to build more awareness of our company and of our products and services? Advocates can help us do that in a number of ways.

- **Fill a need**—Are we trying to address specific needs that have arisen around our products? Perhaps, in the medical example, surgeons are using the equipment beyond its warranty date or patients are experiencing negative effects. Advocates can help us address specific needs.

- **Take action**—Are we hoping/expecting our advocates to take positive action on our behalf, such as write about us in the press or speak on our behalf at industry gatherings?

The way we approach our advocacy strategy will depend on a combination of these two criteria: What are we trying to accomplish, and whom do we want to help us?

MOVING AROUND THE GRID

To plan and execute an advocacy strategy is more complicated than a short book can address, so we won't look at every corner of the grid. But here are a few simple examples.

Let's say we want to create awareness of a new surgical product. The surgeon would be the *user*. So we might want to educate the user by making them aware we have a new tool that will make their surgical process safer, faster, and more effective. We might want to offer them how-to videos or videos of how other surgeons have used the tool successfully. We might want to show them reviews of the features and functions of the tool.

If we move to the far right, though, and we're dealing with the hospital administrator—the *decider*—we must understand that executives don't care about the same things users do. When educating executives, we'll talk about the increase in revenue or the reduction in death rates that will result from using the new tool. If we make the mistake of talking up the tool's technical specs with the hospital administrator, who's never going to use the tool, our efforts will fail.

If a product-related need arises—for instance, the equipment isn't being used properly and is causing problems as a result—we might try to develop power *users* as advocates. For example, we might train one particular surgeon extensively on the tool so that he or she can share their know-how with other surgeons across the department or in neighboring hospitals. Or we might target *influencers*, such as industry analysts, who can write positively about the issue in trade magazines or talk about it in the media.

On the action front, we might want our *users* to become active in user groups, our *influencers* to join our customer advisory board, and our *deciders* to represent our firm in a trade association. In each case, we must target and approach the potential advocate in a structured way with a well-defined path that provides some likely benefits *to them*.

***

Whenever we offer the world a truly great product or service, we *will* get advocates. There will be people who sing our praises. But if we are *deliberate* about cultivating advocacy rather than leaving it all to chance, we can develop even more of these invaluable assets.

Advocacy Best Practices

When designing an advocacy program at your company, strive to keep these ideas in mind:

1. DETERMINE YOUR OVERALL PLAN AND GOALS

Most people don't even think about *planning* their advocacy, they just let it happen and hope for the best. Starting with an actual plan and actual goals will already put us ahead of most of our competitors. We should ask questions such as: *How many advocates do we want to develop this year? How much business do we want to drive from advocacy? Who are the users, influencers, and deciders we want to target in each client company? How?* If we want to cultivate advocates, we need to provide the structure, path, and benefits.

2. CHOOSE THE RIGHT ADVOCATES

It's critical to pour our advocacy efforts into developing the right people. One thing I learned in the restaurant business is that if a customer has a bad experience, they're five times more likely to tell their friends about it than if they have a good one. So we certainly don't want *negative* advocates, those who are going to blast us on social media or complain to the Better Business Bureau. It is important, therefore, to target people who (1) have gained substantial value from our products and (2) have generally positive, cooperative attitudes and personalities.

> I learned in the restaurant business that if a customer has a bad experience, they're five times more likely to tell their friends about it than if they have a good one.

3. USE ADVOCACY AND COLLABORATION SOFTWARE

When our advocacy goals are modest, such as trying to gain a few hundred or a few thousand advocates, we probably don't need to use specialized software; we can track folks in our CRM system. But if we're trying to reach tens of thousands or millions of customers, we will need a lot more advocates. That means we'll need some type of software that addresses not only how to *manage* our advocates but also how to collaborate and engage with them. There are platforms specifically designed for advocacy, such as GaggleAMP, Quorum, or Influitive; there are also generic collaboration platforms like Microsoft Teams and Slack, where team members can engage with each other. When political groups talk about the ground game, they're using software to organize, energize, and empower their legions of supporters.

4. PREPARE ADVOCATES

As we're recruiting advocates, we need to be preparing them, specifically in regard to the things we want them to advocate *for*. We want to exert some direction over the message. In politics, for example, we might want our advocates to zero in on one or two policy points within our bigger platform. If we're in the software business, we might have a new release coming out that we want people to talk about. *Any* advocate is better than no advocate at all, but if a hundred advocates are each talking about something different, that weakens and dilutes their impact.

5. CREATE QUALITY CONTENT

We need to give our advocates the tools and resources with which to advocate for us. Advocates might need, for example, videos, literature, guidebooks, templates, and testimonials, as well as perhaps gifts and free samples to give out. If we're in politics, advocates need to be provided with our policy platform. If we're in technology or if we're selling any kind of tech-based product, advocates need our features list. The higher the quality of material and tools we can arm our advocates with, the better.

6. PROVIDE GUIDANCE TO ADVOCATES

Guidance goes deeper than preparation (#4). *Preparing* our advocates is about setting the table—"Here are some of the things we're doing with our advocacy program"—but guidance is about specifically *directing* our advocates to be good spokespeople for us. This might include providing guidelines for them to communicate advocate-to-advocate as well as advocate-to-consumer. It might include doing some form of informal training or education with them to help them to do their advocating in a way that's consistent with our brand values and sensitive to our clients.

7. REWARDS AND CONTESTS

When possible and appropriate, we should set up reward structures for our advocates—gifts of appreciation, yes, but also rewards and contests based on how many referrals they make for us or how many new customers they help bring in. This might be something simple like a $5 gift card, or it might be something substantial. Sometimes people, by virtue of their employment, aren't allowed to accept material or monetary rewards. In this case, offering professional recognition or reputation-enhancing opportunities such as speaking gigs can be highly rewarding. It's a matter of knowing our industry—what can and can't be done—and being creative within those bounds.

8. EVALUATE RESULTS AND MAKE ADJUSTMENTS

Finally, as in all other steps in the Loop, we must measure our results to make sure that what we're doing is working. And if it isn't, we must make adjustments. Here's where we ask, *How well did we do?* and *What are we going to do differently next cycle?*

Having good KPIs is crucial in this regard. We might try to measure, for example, the extent to which our advocates are influencing revenue. What kind of ROI are we getting? Even though we're not paying advocates a salary, we *are* investing in our advocacy program. Is the investment paying off? When an advocate is affiliated with our product, is our win rate higher or lower than our average? Is our sales cycle shorter when advocates get involved?

Do we have advocates in all of the industries we do business in? Do we have them for all of our business units? For all of our product lines?

There are many ways to quantify what we're doing in the advocacy realm. We need to treat advocacy with the same methodical and programmatic approach we use for the other steps in the Loop. This may require working with professional consultants, but we can start by simply having a plan of attack.

***

Client Expansion—Onboarding, Adoption, Value Realization, Loyalty, and Advocacy—adds a whole new dimension to the Funnel, as you can see. Customers are no longer seen as onetime opportunities to be converted, forgotten, and (perhaps) rewon again in the future but rather as perennial resources with whom we maintain ongoing, dynamic relationships.

Again, these five stages are not tightly prescribed. In the next section, we'll look at how the Loop is meant to be flexible.

PART III
IT'S YOURS NOW

CHAPTER 11

PERSONALIZE
YOUR LOOP

B ack in part I, we saw that many of the Funnel's problems
spring from its rigidity: Funnels aren't able to adapt to
different companies or customers, and they're benchmarked against other businesses that are nothing like
our own. When we force our business into a model it wasn't designed
for, just in order to benchmark ourselves, what do the benchmarks
even mean?

In part II, we encountered a new marketing model: the Loop. I
told you the Loop was an improved model because it better reflected
the customer experience and was designed for nurturing *long-term
relationships* with clients rather than closed-ended transactions.

And then we looked at some of the stages the Loop often encompasses. At this point, a red flag might have flashed for you. Despite my assurances otherwise, you might now be wondering: Isn't the Loop, with all of its steps, just as rigid as the Funnel? And haven't we simply replaced the movement of gravity with a repetitive looping motion?

The short answer is no. The longer answer is … well, what part III is about.

Here we'll begin to explore what it takes to adopt, operationalize, and implement the Loop model. In other words, how to *personalize* it and make it work for us. We'll discover how the Loop model can morph to fit our company, as well as how it can account for the realities of various types of customer experience.

Let's start there: with the customer experience …

A New Metaphor: A Slow, Meandering River

Built into the Funnel model is an assumption of gravitational force—that once our leads begin to consider us, they will move in one direction only: toward us. But that's not what the buying experience actually looks like from the customer side. Chutes and Ladders, remember? Real customers don't only slide down chutes *toward* us; they also climb up ladders *away* from us.

They pause, they change their minds, they visit a competitor, they revamp their plans.

An authentic courtship between marketers and customers must allow for these qualities of ebb and flow. The reason we proposed the Loop versus the Funnel is that we want to be able to go in multiple directions—back and forth, side to side, and in and out, not only from top to bottom.

To personalize the Loop means to reflect how our customers are *actually* buying and to recognize they may be taking many different paths to a purchase. Of course, we all *want* to advance the sale in a Funnel-like way. But what do we do when the buyer is not ready? What happens if the buyer wants to go backward, change directions, go onto a whole different assembly line? Can we accommodate all those paths?

The Funnel is a waterfall that rushes powerfully in one direction. The Loop, on the other hand, can be thought of as a lazy, meandering river. This lazy river has a natural flow pattern, but not everyone will follow that flow. Customers can get on where they want and get off where they want. Everyone can have *their own experience* of the river.

Sure, some folks will stay in the lazy river and let it carry them from start to finish, around and around, but others might get out, buy a hot dog, grab a beer, and head back to the start. Or they might stroll downstream. Some might cross the river and get off on the other side. Some might row against the current for a while. Some might stay on the river all day long, take a nap, read a book. Some might want to get off after one stop.

> **The idea of the Loop is to find out what kind of experience your customers prefer and to design a river journey that matches their preferred behavior.**

The idea is to find out what kind of experience your customers prefer and to design a river journey that matches their preferred behavior.

Numbers of Loops and Stages

The Loop is a metaphor, a loose model, not a rigid system. The stages of the Loop aren't prescriptive. They exist only to provide conceptual clarity: here are the main phases a customer *might* pass through over time. But the customer's *actual* experience of the Loop will probably involve some moments of going backward, taking lateral steps, or skipping ahead.

We don't even need to use one single Loop. We can use multiple Loops. What if, for example, we sell three products—a transactional product, a midbusiness product, and an enterprise product? These three products might have very different price points and very different purchase trajectories.

A transactional product typically has a very short and simple sales cycle, with few consults needed. As an example from domestic life, you and your spouse can both go out and buy a loaf of bread on your own. You don't need to consult with each other. Buying bread is a transaction. You just do it. But when it comes to your retirement plan, your house, or a new car, that's a different matter. Wholly different purchasing experience. Wholly different steps.

Similarly, in business, a manager might have the authority to schedule a cleaning service or buy a small software product or a new coffee maker in a simple transactional way. They have a budget, they can put their purchase on a procurement card, they don't need to check with anyone. The whole cycle might take a few hours, a few days, a week, maybe a month.

But when it comes to an enterprise purchase—something that affects the whole business—we might be looking at three, six, twelve, or twenty-four-month sales cycles. Ten or fifteen people within the company might need to be involved. When a customer is buying a two-hundred-thousand-dollar software solution or medical equipment that costs a million bucks, they're not making that purchase alone. They have multiple people on their decision team. They are evaluating multiple vendors. They are doing a risk/reward analysis. They are checking references, conducting due diligence, negotiating complex contracts. A very different buying cycle.

So we may need to use multiple Loops. Or maybe we use one Loop, but we think carefully about the entire customer experience and how our client company uses our different products and experiences *together*. It really depends on what we're selling and whom we're selling to. Every company's Loop can (and should) look a bit different.

Similarly, there's no law saying there can't be more or fewer then ten stages. One company and its customers might need six steps, while another company and *its* customers might need fifteen. The number of stages might be different for the different products we offer. In some cases, we might need to add, for example, a justification step, a proof of concept step, a trial period step, or a board approval step to the Client Acquisition side. Or we might need to combine consideration and evaluation together.

On the Client Expansion side, we might need to add, subtract, or combine steps as well. If we're in a transactional service like a hotel or restaurant, for example, separating onboarding and adoption into two stages may not make sense because the customer experience happens so quickly. Sometimes we might need to call stages by different names to fit the client company's nomenclature or mindset.

Ultimately, if we decide to have three steps on the left and seventeen on the right or vice versa, it doesn't matter. The stages are just a representation. It's what we're *doing* in the stages that matters. Sales and marketing must be doing specific things within each of those stages that line up with what the customer needs at that particular time. The paradigm shift from the Funnel to the Loop is really about becoming more customer centric.

So What *Does* the Customer Need?

How can we determine what our customers' actual experiences look like so that we can address and enhance those experiences with the right approach?

Once again, we can ask the customer.

ASK

So many businesses try to capture their customers' experiences by sending out surveys once or twice a year. We talked about this earlier. Surveys often don't work because they ask the wrong questions. *How likely are you to recommend us to a friend? How happy are you with our product or service?* Okay, so we receive a three out of five on the happiness meter; what does that really tell us? What do we *do* with that information?

A slightly better survey question would be, *Is there anything we could be doing better now?* That at least elicits a specific response from the customer. Even better is to ask concrete questions like: *What problems are you trying to solve with our product/service? What are the top three things you would change about our product? What are the top three things you get value from? What did you think our product would do that it's not doing? What is our product doing that you didn't expect? Do you feel what you're paying is fair for the value you're getting?*

But just as a Funnel can't replace a real relationship, a survey can't replace a real conversation. Far better to get our customers on the phone, invite them to our office, sit them down with our team to share their experiences, good and bad.

Jeff Bezos famously keeps an empty chair open at every executive meeting to represent the customer. Even better, he often brings in real customers to fill that seat.

Everyone wants to be the next Amazon or Netflix. What many people don't realize is that these services were built around the customer from the beginning. That's why you can start watching a Netflix show on your television, continue it on your laptop, and finish it on your phone. That's how Netflix became the better-mousetrap version of the video store in the first place—by continually asking the customer what would make their experience better.

We in marketing need to get out of our ivory-tower offices and go out and visit customers. We need to ask them real questions, not just make assumptions. Instead of sitting in a room with our peers coming up with the next great marketing campaign, we should be finding out whether or not what we're doing is working with real people.

One way to dip our toes in these waters is simply to put marketers on sales calls. That's a surprisingly rare practice, and yet it's a great way to ensure that our team is looking past the theoretical narratives and connecting with the realities of the customer experience.

OBSERVE AND MONITOR

In addition to talking to our customers, we should also be observing what they're *actually doing*. If we're in the software business, we can check to see what features they're using, how many users are logging in, and how often. In a financial services company, we can check on how often the client is meeting with their advisor and whether their portfolio is growing at a rate above or below those of other clients. With modern automobiles, there are built-in monitoring systems that allow car companies to see if customers are driving their cars properly. Data about how clients are actually using our products are vital.

LOOK AT OBJECTIVE DATA TOO

Data about the real world is also crucial. Often marketers will get together in a room and dream up personas and hypothetical buyer journeys. But all that conjecture is born of *assumptions*. Models need to reflect actual realities instead. We need to look at all the available data to learn about the actual personas and behaviors of actual buyers.

Consider, for example, looking at:

- Third-party market research

- Data analysis

- Records of digital behavior

- TV analytics

- Social media analytics

- Company website data

- Financial data

- Government trends

- Search engine trends

- Spending data
- Customer service records
- Demographic information
- Industry trends (in various industries, not just our own)

Digging into such sources will help you prove, disprove, and augment the assumptions you might be relying on about your customers and their experiences. Ultimately, it will help you build a better customized Loop for your business: one that ensures a close, authentic relationship between you and your customers.

***

We should never bend over backward to make our business conform to a particular marketing model. Rather, we should find and customize a marketing model that looks like our business.

> **We should find and customize a marketing model that looks like our business.**

Once we've taken the Loop and made it our own, we can begin digitizing it and measuring its performance. But first let's start by talking about how successful companies *manage* their Loops ...

CHAPTER 12

MANAGE YOUR LOOP

W hatever business we're in, and no matter what department, we put systems, processes, and procedures in place to manage our company so that we can be more efficient, more effective, more productive. We refine these systems over time so that they work even more efficiently.

But these management controls are usually designed through a company lens, right? And the questions we ask are *filtered* through that lens. How much overtime are we using? How much time are employees spending on the phone? How much extra staffing will we need this holiday season?

We ask mostly company-centric questions, questions about

managing the company itself. And we put company-centric measures in place to answer them. Nothing wrong with that. All companies need internal systems and processes.

But when we decide to use the Loop, we are making a conscious decision to take a *customer*-centric approach. That means we are now in the business of *relationship management.* That means, in turn, that we'll be managing things differently than we were before. We'll be looking *to the client* for our cues about what to do next. Where is each client on the Loop? What is their experience right now? What can we do to improve this part of their journey? Where are we falling down? What will they be needing from us next?

Our entire role in the company becomes one of servicing our customer/client relationships. Just as the Funnel was a mechanism to assemble more leads, the Loop is a mechanism to build better customer relationships.

Linear vs. "Organic"

As I've said before, the Funnel fits in well with a company-centric, assembly-line type of approach. Funnel thinking is linear, unidirectional, and simple. Its focus is narrow: What can we do to generate more leads and convert more leads into sales? It's all about the numbers.

"Loop thinking" is more organic, more holistic, more open ended. Our efforts are dictated by what is going on with our customers, not by our model. Shape-wise, Loop-style management is more amoeba-like; we flow our attention toward wherever it is needed by the customer. The Loop is simply a structure we use to remind ourselves of the many things we need to be doing year-round to tend to our customer relationships. Our *actions*, however, are always based on where the customer is actually at right now.

Relationship management is proactive, not reactive. That means most of our energy goes into (1) understanding where our customers are on the Loop (they may be at multiple stages), (2) finding out what they need from us to have a better experience wherever they're at, and (3) creatively delivering on those needs.

To manage this kind of scenario requires viewing things through a different lens and using a wholly different management approach. Instead of pouring customers through our Funnel, *we* reach out to *them* based on anticipating and assessing their current needs. The approach we use is fundamentally more fluid and creative.

Different Conversations

Relationship management starts by having a different set of conversations from the ones we're normally used to. These conversations provide the key to the types of actions we should be taking and the types of roles, structures, and expectations we should be putting in place.

FUNNEL CONVERSATIONS	LOOP CONVERSATIONS
How many bookings have we done this year to date? What's in the pipeline? What's going to close next week? We need more leads. We need more customers. *(Rinse and repeat.)*	What's been the average utilization of our products and services? How many new advocates have we generated? What percentage of our customers are realizing value from our products or services?
How many prospects viewed our demo? How many demos converted to a sale? How can we improve that conversion rate?	Did the people who viewed the demo get their questions answered? Did they need to watch multiple demos? How long did they stay engaged with the demo? Did they ask follow-up questions? Did they ask for additional information after the demo?
The customer closed the deal, great. They come up for renewal a year from now. So we'll just reach out to them thirty to ninety days before the contract expires and renew them.	Let's set up periodic touchpoints throughout the year to make sure our customer is happy and they're actively using our product or service. If we do our job right, then when it comes time to renew, we won't even *have* to ask them; they'll be asking us. *They'll* take the action, and that action will flow naturally out of all the things we've been doing *for* and *with* them all year.

FUNNEL CONVERSATIONS	LOOP CONVERSATIONS
Our customer service is fine. We've got a hotline customers can call if they're having trouble with our products. We've got a complaint line too. We sent out customer surveys, and most of the ones that were returned (okay, that was only 28 percent of them, but still) say our customers are happy.	Let's hold the client's hand throughout the whole installation/initiation period. Let's check back with them in a few days and make sure they know how to use all the features. Let's monitor them and talk to them regularly to make sure they're *actually using* all the features and getting benefits from them …
We need to win this account. Your go-to guy at the client company seems to be on the fence. Go wine him and dine him, offer him another 5 percent off, but give him a time limit on the deal. Get him to say yes before the quarter ends!	We need to understand the makeup of the whole decision-making *team*. We need to reach out to influential users, purchasers, and executives within the company and educate them, answer their concerns. Only if the whole company is behind us will we develop a strong, ongoing client relationship.

Based on such conversations, our management approach will obviously change. Back in the Funnel days—when our whole focus was centered around generating leads, getting people in the pipeline, and closing deals—we could rely on a predictable range of action options: throw more salespeople out there, revise our literature, reevaluate our pricing structure … But when we start having customer-centric conversations, we can be led in innumerable directions.

Management Action Options

WHEN YOU START WITH THE FUNNEL

1. AWARENESS

- Improve content marketing
- Build social media presence
- Create new ad campaign

2. INTEREST

- Create new landing page
- Develop case studies
- Launch email marketing campaign
- Improve web content

3. DECISION

- Improve sales page
- Write and send proposals
- Do time-limited offer

4. ACTION

- Streamline payment system
- Improve shopping cart/credit card interface
- Publish ratings and reviews

WHEN YOU START WITH A CUSTOMER-CENTRIC QUESTION

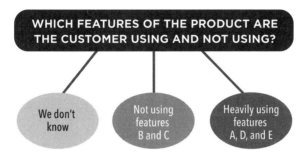

WHICH FEATURES OF THE PRODUCT ARE THE CUSTOMER USING AND NOT USING?

- We don't know
- Not using features B and C
- Heavily using features A, D, and E

EXAMPLE: WHICH FEATURES OF THE PRODUCT ARE THE CUSTOMER USING AND NOT USING?

1. WE DON'T KNOW

- Improve our monitoring process
  - Add better software reporting
  - Assign Adoption Manager to do weekly follow-ups with customer
  - Schedule staff training on importance of full adoption

2. NOT USING FEATURES B AND C

- Meet with key executives to explain revenue benefits of features B & C
- Develop better training process for customer on product features
  - Review competitors' literature
  - Change trainer position to full-time
- Meet with key users to determine why they don't like/use features B & C

3. HEAVILY USING FEATURES A, D, AND E

- Send out "super user" congratulations letter
- Offer surprise reward for key users
  - Brainstorm ideas at next staff meeting
- Identify potential advocates within heavy-user group

The type of mindset and approach shown in the customer-centric version produces a much broader perspective on the customer than simply asking, "Can we get more leads or not?" If we follow the path of the customer, we might decide to do things like create innovational apps or try product accelerators. We might want to set up trial groups at new points in the process and install new feedback mechanisms. Rather than staying locked into the traditional structure of sales team, service team, manufacturing plant, and call center, we might create hybrid departments that better align with customers' needs and experiences.

We might even create new *roles*, such as a chief customer officer. This might lead to thinking about our whole work structure differently. Maybe we'll create a whole department focused on customer success and innovation. Maybe we'll design new compensation plans that award bonuses based on customer-centricity, not just pure business performance.

In short, *we* adapt our company to serving the customer; the customer does not adapt to serving *us*. Are you getting how profound a change this is?

Different Impact

As I've said before—and want to stress again—implementing the Loop is not a light and casual decision. It affects every aspect of the organization and requires the active participation of the entire company. As we're managing the Loop, we must keep in mind the various ways in which the Loop can impact key entities.

HOW DOES THE LOOP IMPACT
THESE FOUR ENTITIES?

Marketing

1. Content is personalized at scale–focused on customer needs and where they are in their buying journey.

2. Program budget is rebalanced to address customer engagement and expansion, not just acquisition.

3. Marketing becomes a revenue center and gains authority and credibility.

4. Marketing becomes a change agent.

5. Resources expand.

6. Better career security is achieved.

7. Technology is more effectively leveraged to address the entire buying cycle, not just acquisition.

8. Marketing now seeks to:

   ▫ Increase Loyalty: Establish deeper, more meaningful connections with its customers by tailoring its messaging and offers to their needs–and keep them coming back long after their first purchase.

   ▫ Increase Efficiency: Invest in the acquisition channels, campaigns, and partners that will help it acquire high-value customers. Avoid costly "batch and blast" discounts by using promotions only when they're needed–for the right shoppers and at crucial moments in the customer life cycle.

   ▫ Increase Agility: Engage with customers at the right time, on the platform that's most relevant to them, with the message that's most likely to resonate at any given moment in time. Be prepared to react rapidly to changes in customers' behavior or preferences.

   ▫ Increase Differentiation: Stand out in a crowded marketplace by moving past generic offers and messaging. Capture and maintain mindshare through a personalized approach.

Sales

1. The sales process is completely different when reimagined around the customer in a digital world.

2. Sales enablement becomes a critical competitive differentiator.

3. New skills are developed around digital enablement, coaching, and facilitation.

4. A greater emphasis is placed on building customer relationships and a customer portfolio than on quotas alone.

5. However, sales actually achieves a greater percentage of its quotas.

6. Turnover decreases.

7. Revenue increases.

8. Salespeople are hired in part based on their empathy skills.

Company

1. Repeatable, predictable, and scalable revenue can be attained. Market share, operating margins, and profits are increased.

2. Business processes, organizational structures, technology, and KPIs are reimagined and oriented around the customer, not around products or business units.

3. Innovation accelerates.

4. Costs to serve are reduced. Operational efficiency and effectiveness are improved.

5. Strategic capabilities are developed around digital transformation, customer-centricity, revenue marketing, change management, and innovation.

6. Customer capabilities are developed around 360-degree engagement, customer experience, demand management, content marketing, brand, and creative.

7. People capabilities are developed around organizational strategy and design, talent management, stakeholder alignment, Marketing and Sales enablement, and cross-functional collaboration.

8. Revenue-operations capabilities are developed around marketing operations, sales operations, customer operations, buyer management, and analytics.

9. Data and technology capabilities are developed around customer engagement architecture, data management and governance, data integration architecture, technology management and optimization, and emerging technology.

Client

1. The client has a consistent, seamless, and memorable experience with the company.

2. Clients become loyalists and advocates.

3. Year over year customer spending increases.

4. Renewal rates increase.

5. Greater value is realized.

6. Efficiency and effectiveness are improved.

7. Higher ROI is achieved.

8. Client satisfaction goes up.

9. The client has a unique experience.

Business Meetings in the Loop

If you've ever sat through a sales and marketing meeting, you know the drill: celebrate the wins, review sales activity, do a pipeline update, talk about new prospects and leads. Blah, blah. One meeting the same as the next. When we use the Loop as our map, however, business meetings become dynamic, creative exchanges in which we push ourselves to new service heights.

Some of the key business tasks we can tackle at Loop-driven meetings include:

1. **Designing custom Loops for clients.** As noted in the last chapter, the Loop is not a mold into which we cram our customers. It is flexible. Some clients may need multiple Loops; some may need steps added to or removed from their Loops. Coming together as a team and planning customized Loop journeys for new and existing clients is a great use of management meetings.

2. **Reviewing clients' Loop requirements.** At every meeting, we can look in detail at one or more clients and discuss how their Loop journey is going. Where are they on the Loop? What do they need from us right now? What could we provide that would be of value? Maybe the client is in the adoption stage with two of our products, the advocacy stage with another, and the Onboarding stage with a fourth. Are we doing everything we can for each product journey?

3. **Doing top-down reviews of our client mix.** With the Loop as our conceptual framework, we can review our entire client mix against our resources and make needed adjustments. For example, if we see that 45 percent of our clients are in the Adoption stage due to a recent product release, we can ask,

"Do we have sufficient resources to address this? Do we need to create an adoption team and put ten people on it for the next two months?"

Handling the Client Mix

Managing our client mix *as a whole* becomes a far greater challenge when we view all our clients as ongoing relationships. Relationships, after all, are more complicated to manage than leads in a pipeline. And the Loop, if used too rigidly and literally, could present a logistical problem: we could end up investing in lots of relationships that just aren't there anymore.

So how do we strike a balance between investing in long-term relationships and shepherding our resources efficiently? How do we ensure that the relationships we invest in are mutual ones?

Many companies take a reductive approach to this challenge. For instance, they might do an eighty-twenty split—"Twenty percent of our customers bring in 80 percent of our revenue, so we'll distribute our energies according to the same ratio." Or they might break down customers into categories of big, medium, and small. But these are rigid, nonadaptive, one-size-fits-all methods. They don't account for the nuances of our individual company and its customers.

Of course it goes without saying that if one customer is more impactful to our business than others, we're going to want to devote more resources and attention to that client. But looking at customers purely in terms of revenue might not tell the whole story. We might have other customers that are bringing in less revenue, but they might be far more profitable, or they might be in an industry or segment that is showing much higher growth.

On the other hand, we might have a customer that's a cash cow at the moment, but their industry may be dying off rapidly. So they could be at risk in a year or two.

So while we're being customer centric and pursuing healthy clients for life, we also have to recognize that not every client can be a lifetime client. We need to have mechanisms in place for determining which clients are healthy for *right now* and which may be healthy over the long term.

My recommendation is to take an approach called "customer portfolio management."

Customer Portfolio Management

The idea behind customer portfolio management—at least as I define it—is to manage our customers like we manage our stock portfolio. That means not looking at customers purely in terms of dollar revenue. It means looking at risk/reward, rates of growth, market sectors, time frame of expected return, and other factors.

Essentially, we can take all the advice a financial manager would give us about maintaining a healthy stock portfolio and apply it to maintaining a healthy customer portfolio.

THE OVERALL MIX IS WHAT MATTERS MOST

Investors often become overly focused on individual stocks in their portfolio, but that's a myopic and risky perspective. What matters most is the overall mix of stocks. The same is true in customer portfolio management. We want a robust mix of high-risk vs. low-risk, long-term vs. short-term, and high-revenue vs. high-profit clients that balance one another in terms of the risk/reward criteria that we deem important to our company. Balance is the key.

DIVERSIFY

A cornerstone of long-term investing is diversification: don't put all your eggs in one enticing basket. Similarly, in a customer portfolio, we don't want to pour all our resources into one or two major clients. Nor do we want to concentrate on a single sector or subsector. There's a saying "there's riches in niches," but that may not be sustainable over the long haul. Niches can change. For instance, what if all our clients are in the travel hospitality industry, and then COVID-19 hits, shutting travel down? If travel's our only segment, we're out of business.

KNOW YOUR RISK TOLERANCE

A general investing principle is that the higher the return you are seeking and the shorter the time frame you have, the higher the risk. Similarly, if we're trying to land a huge client and we want to gain quick and substantial profit from that client—say, *this quarter*—we may be tempted to pour all of our resources into landing that client. That's high risk. What if we fail? Do we have enough other clients in healthy shape that we'll be okay financially? As in stock investing, we never want to risk more than we can comfortably afford to lose. An investment manager will often segment a portfolio into "buckets": a short-term/high-risk bucket; a medium-term/medium-risk bucket; and a long-term/low-risk bucket. The risks/returns of each bucket work to offset one another. We can and should do the same with customers.

KNOW WHEN TO HOLD 'EM, KNOW WHEN TO FOLD 'EM

As investors, we're cautioned to put our faith in well-researched stocks, to hold them long term and not sell them at the first sign of market volatility. Similarly, when we have developed a promising client, we should continue investing in that relationship even if it doesn't look like it will bear new fruit immediately and even if there are setbacks. I've heard stories of teams that wooed companies for years and then "suddenly" received multimillion-dollar contracts from them. At the same time, like an investment manager, we must ensure that the premises that caused us to make the investment in the first place remain valid. Sometimes big things change, and we have to cut our losses by letting go of clients that are never going to bring us business.

DON'T LET EMOTION RUN THE SHOW

Both the fear of loss and the excitement of easy gains can trigger us to do foolish things with our stock portfolios. Similar emotions can cause us to prematurely abandon good customer relations strategies—and good customers—and go chasing shiny new objects. Remain detached, stay the course, and make changes thoughtfully, not impulsively.

If we think of our customer relationships as investments—which they are—we gain a helpful perspective by which to manage them.

CHAPTER 13

MEASURE AND DIGITIZE YOUR LOOP

What isn't measured isn't managed is a business maxim I'm sure you've heard once or twice. As we're thinking about managing our Loop, it is a maxim worth repeating.

Data is vital. In order to determine how best to invest our energy in each customer, we need to collect data to tell us (1) what needs to be done next for the customer and (2) whether what we're *currently* doing is working. Otherwise everything remains nebulous and vague.

Even the *attempt* to measure is a good thing. It forces us into greater specificity. "Improving customer relationships," for example, is a meaningless goal to aim for. Too vague. It can't be measured or managed. However, "reducing calls to the complaint line by 50 percent" *can* be measured and also suggests the beginnings of a game plan.

In addition to measuring, we also need to use good digital tools to help us *manage* the Loop. Digital tools are essential in this day and age. The problem is, there are approximately seventeen bajillion digital tools out there and counting. How do we know the right ones to use?

The answer, put simply, lies in customer-centricity. When it comes to measuring and digitizing, we can either go tech centric or customer centric. Going tech centric (which most companies do) leads us into a hornet's nest; going customer centric gives us a road map to follow.

We'll talk only briefly about measuring and digitizing in this book. Otherwise we run the risk of becoming highly technical and, well, boring. My goal here is just to offer you a way of thinking about technological matters so that when you're ready to bring in the experts, you'll be thinking in the right direction.

Measure

The marketing consulting world is in love with stats and benchmarks. If you spend any time with consultants, you will be drawn into their systems for measuring all sorts of variables and for benchmarking your scores against those of other companies. But just because something *can* be measured doesn't mean it *should* be measured.

> **Just because something *can* be measured doesn't mean it *should* be measured.**

MEASURE THE RIGHT THINGS

Many years ago, when I was just getting started in the marketing space, I was a dedicated techie and stat nerd. I came up with dozens and dozens of metrics and KPIs that I thought would be really helpful to measure marketing performance. Some of them were quite creative and clever. And so, having dutifully assembled my list, I proudly sat down with the CFO of the company to show the list to him. He just shook his head and said, "Jeff, I don't need any of these numbers to know how well marketing's doing. I just need one."

"What's that?" I said.

He replied, "Return on marketing investment. I look at how much money I gave you last year and how much revenue we generated against that spending. Then I look at the same thing this year. If your number went up, that tells me you're doing a better job. If the number was flat or went down, that means you didn't do as good a job, so you get less money."

An oversimplification? Perhaps. But it was eye opening for me because I think people too often get caught up in trying to measure everything. Or they spend their time measuring the wrong things. They're not really looking at what's most important for *their particular* company and *their particular* customers. They're looking at what their peers are doing and at what the technology is set up to measure. They're looking at what they learned in business school.

Today we can build dashboards for anything. We can create Excel spreadsheets, pie charts, tables, and graphs using beautiful, colorful imagery. And it's easy to fall in love with all that cool stuff—after all, we paid good money for the software. It's easy to get lured into paying more attention to the *tools* than to the stuff the tools are supposed to be measuring.

But ultimately, what's the question we're trying to answer? What are we really trying to measure? What is the key data that's going to tell us whether we're being more customer centric than not? Far better to look at one, two, or three key measures that get to the heart of where things stand with our customers than to look at seventy-five things that give us only peripheral or supportive information. For example, finding out how many users at the client company were actively employing "feature x" of our software last month—and for how many hours—may tell us more about how the Adoption phase is going than all other stats combined.

Not that the other standard metrics don't matter—supportive information has its place—but sometimes we can miss the forest for the trees unless we're concentrating on the few things that are going to give us *directional* insight on whether or not we're doing things right.

MEASURE FOR YOUR AUDIENCE

When deciding what key measurements to track and communicate, we need to think about our audience too. Instead of inundating everyone in our company with excess data that makes their eyes glaze over, we should be selective and targeted. We should communicate to each person only the data they need to see, only the data that means something to *them*, and only the data that strategically helps the company achieve its goals (i.e., serving the customer) *through* them.

So at a board or CEO level, we might be tracking and communicating strategic elements like return on spending, margin, lifetime customer value, and so on. At a CFO level, we'll be looking at revenue and costs, etc. At a campaign or field level, where things are more tactical, we might be interested in traffic, impressions, number of leads, that type of thing. And so, depending on what audience we're communicating with, we create different types of dashboards and reports. Give people only the two or three pieces of data that matter to them and can help them make customer-centric decisions.

MEASURE FOR YOUR BUSINESS MODEL

The things we should be measuring are only those things that make sense for *our* business model. Measuring customer attrition rates, for example, makes no sense if our business has only five main customers and we know them all intimately. We need to measure what matters to the way *our business works.* That may entail creating whole new terms and concepts rather than looking at traditional measures that don't really apply.

Twenty years ago, for example, people didn't really talk about churn or attrition, monthly recurring revenue, or annual recurring revenue. People didn't hire customer success managers. These concepts arose when the subscription model came into vogue as a new business model for selling software. Before the 2000s, if you bought software, it shipped in a box with DVDs, CDs, or floppy disks, and it was physically installed on premise. Or it was preinstalled on a mainframe. You paid multiyear or perpetual license fees. But cloud computing and the subscription model changed all that. Now you rent access to the platform. You own the data, but you don't own the software. With this new business model, companies began to name and measure different things.

What key elements do you need to name and measure for your unique business?

MEASURE FOR THE LOOP

Using the Loop means measuring new things. The Loop is a completely different approach to engaging with customers and driving demand. Once we decide the Funnel's not right for us anymore and we want to adopt the Loop, we need to make a radical change in our thinking. We're now enhancing relationships, not managing assembly lines. And that means we can't measure only the same old things we measured in the Funnel days. If we do, we're not going to get the right set of outcomes. We're not going to make the right decisions.

Many companies have systems in place for measuring the five stages of Customer Acquisition, but most don't have processes established for measuring performance in Customer Expansion. That's where we need to get creative. We need to ask: What does our customer need and want at each of the five stages of Customer Expansion (or whatever number of stages we're using), and how can we measure our alignment with those desires?

The things we measure at each stage in our Customer Expansion cycle should be tailored to *our unique business* and *our unique customers*—I can't stress that point enough—but here are some examples of things we might want to look at:

- **Onboarding**—Look at time to adoption, content engagement figures, number of client-initiated calls vs. company-initiated calls.

- **Adoption**—Try to measure product/service utilization, benefits realization rates, change failure rates, user satisfaction levels.

- **Value Realization**—Look at process efficiency and effectiveness, business value gained from new methods, customer financial performance and market share performance, customer return on investment (CAPEX and OPEX).

- **Loyalty**—Pay attention to customer attrition and retention rates, customer lifetime value (LCV), customer wallet share, customer participation, customer price elasticity, relationship value maturity.

- **Advocacy**—Try to measure influenced revenue, influence-to-win ratios, win rates, sales cycle compression, advocates added.

At each stage, what are the one or two key pieces of data that will keep us on track to providing a great customer experience? Focus on those.

Digitize

Today good digital tools are also an essential part of managing customer relationships. But how do we know the best tools to employ, especially when there is *so* much technology available?

Fifteen years ago there might have been fifty applications that dealt with sales and marketing. Today we have almost *ten thousand* such software tools. An average large enterprise that brings in a billion-plus dollars in revenue often has over *two hundred* different technologies that it uses across sales, marketing, and service. Medium-sized businesses (in, say, the hundred million- to billion-dollar range) can have over a hundred, and even SMBs may have forty or fifty different systems.

So how do we even begin to know which tools to use? Well, of course, the answer to such complexity can't be found in one chapter of a marketing book, but the compass we can use, again, is customer-centricity.

PUT THE CUSTOMER IN THE MIDDLE

One of the big mistakes people make when digitizing anything is they don't think about the customer at all. Everyone in the company buys technology to run their own department and handle their own department's concerns. Then they wonder why they can't get a consolidated view of the customer. Marketing buys a marketing platform so it can market to prospects via email campaigns. But the marketing folks aren't thinking about how to use their technology with *current* customers. Why? Because that's not their department. The customer service team, for its part, runs out and buys some service management software to manage *its* cases. Sales runs its prospecting system, billing runs *its* system ...

And that's how we end up with a situation, like I mentioned earlier, in which a customer calls in with an issue and has to repeat their name, account number, and presenting problem five different times to five different departments, and then the call gets dropped, and they have to start all over again. Or where a marketing team sends out an email to every prospect, no matter how inappropriate, because it doesn't have customized prospect data in its particular system. Or where a service department may maintain a great record of customer preferences, but the people who answer the phone don't have access to those records.

The point is this: when we digitize, we're not trying to manage multiple parallel assembly lines. We're trying to build a bridge to our customer. That means we literally have to *put the customer in the middle of the paper* and then *draw the systems we need around them* in order to connect us to them and give them a great customer experience.

To envision what it's like to put the customer in the middle of the technology stack, think about Uber. When Uber began, it had a huge problem to solve. Customers were not used to getting into nontaxicab vehicles with unprofessional drivers, and so Uber had to overcome some initial resistance. To do this, it created a customer-centric experience so seamless and convenient it was a no-brainer for customers to choose Ubers over taxis. It built multiple technologies *around the customer* in a single app that enabled such functions as booking a ride, making payments, geolocation and mapping, traffic estimation, live messaging, push notifications, price calculations (that change dynamically), driver ratings, driver identification, autocalculated tipping, and more. Customer in the middle, tech serving customer.

Netflix didn't say, *How do we build a great content management system for our content? How do we build a good subscription system for our subscribers? How do we build a good advertising system for our advertisers?* No. It built its systems in an integrated way around the customer.

Again, it's a question of customer centric versus tech centric. When we let the technology drive the bus, everyone's playing a game of whack-a-mole, putting out fires, trying to figure out how to get systems to talk to each other. No one's taking care of the customer. Or if they are, they're forcing the customer to adapt to *their* technology rather than making their technology serve the customer. Technology needs to be implemented with a purpose. And that purpose must be a better customer experience.

USE TWO MAIN SYSTEMS, THEN CUSTOMIZE

When it comes to digitizing, there are two main systems we need to deploy nowadays in order to successfully run a business that markets and sells to numerous customers. After that, we can build any additionally needed technology around the customer in a tailored way.

Customer Relationship Management

A modern customer relationship management (CRM) system is a necessity today, whether it's Salesforce, Microsoft Dynamics, Oracle, SAP, or one of the other many CRM solutions. CRM is the system sales uses to manage the opportunity life cycle. CRM is also used to store information about accounts and contacts, leads, and pipeline. Depending upon the platform, it can do a lot more. It might also keep records of customer service calls, it might have commerce included in it, etc.; it can potentially be an end-to-end platform to provide you all the critical information you need to address your customers.

Marketing Automation Platform

Marketing automation technology is also important, whether it's part of a CRM system or a separate (but integrated) system. This platform should have journey orchestration capabilities—meaning it should allow us to orchestrate exactly what we want to happen in our marketing communications.

Essentially, we set up a customized set of if/then parameters, much like an adventure game on a computer. For example: We send Bob an email. *If* he opens the email, we wait two days and send him a text message. If he responds to the text, we send him a direct mail package. If he *doesn't* open the email, we send another email. If he doesn't respond to email number two, we call him. That kind of thing. We orchestrate a series of communication touches so that the customer receives the right messages and content from us at the right time and the right place.

With those two systems in place, plus some type of reporting capability, we can run the entire Loop.

Other Tech

There are many other technologies that can optimize adoption of the Loop—depending on our needs and our customers—but they're not hard requirements. For example, if we're selling strategically and taking an account-based marketing approach, a platform like 6sense or Demandbase can help. These platforms collect information about companies from all over the web. They can provide key information on our ideal customer profile and which companies are in the market for our products and services and which ones aren't.

Imagine you're running a furniture store. I walk into your store to browse, but you don't know how many other furniture stores I've been to first, or how many others I'm planning to go to, or what I'm in the market for. Imagine, though, if you knew *before I arrived* that I was shopping for a new office set, and you could dynamically arrange your furniture store so that as soon as I came in the door, the first displays I saw were for office furniture? This isn't possible in the brick-and-mortar world, but it is absolutely possible to do it digitally.

This is the type of technology that allows Amazon to show *me* the latest thriller when I open its site but show *you* the latest romance novel. The more we know about our customers, the more we can start setting up a tailored experience for them from the moment they first visit us.

> **The more we know about our customers, the more we can start setting up a tailored experience for them from the moment they first visit us.**

We might also want to employ social engagement, advocacy, or employee amplification software, for example. We can mix and match depending upon what outcome we're trying to achieve.

And solutions don't need to be limited to software. They can and should be people based as well. It's all a matter of taking the time to really think about what our customer needs, how they buy, and what they want.

Bottom line: There's no need to go out and buy all the latest software tools. Rather, we should design our processes around the customer. We should max out what our current systems—manual and digital—can handle, and then, when we figure out where the gaps are, go buy the next system. Tech should be serving us and our customers, not driving the bus.

***

So here in part III we've been looking at what it takes to make the Loop our own and operationalize it. But this whole time we've been telling a bit of a lie—a lie of omission. We've been behaving as though it's possible for our marketing department to execute on all of these strategies alone. But as we'll see in part IV, that's far from the case.

PART IV

THE LOOP IS NOT AN ISLAND

CHAPTER 14

COURTING CHANGE

U p until now, we've been talking about the philosophical shifts and practical actions marketing teams can take to build better relationships with their customers. But the reality is that a marketing department can't do any of this work alone. In order to implement the Loop in a meaningful way, we need to get our whole company aligned.

And that isn't always an easy thing to do.

The kind of change we're talking about here isn't the modest kind, like adding a new level to the organizational structure or porting the company over to a new software platform. To implement the Loop is to embrace a seismic shift in behavior. And changes of behavior are profoundly challenging.

FthiForFunnel

Think about how long it took to break people of the habit of smoking in public buildings or to learn the habit of wearing seatbelts. Think about the adoption of email, texting, social media, and e-commerce. People are slow to change behavior, even when the change is good for them.

And so that's the challenge this fourth and final part of the book will address.

What does it take to inspire company-wide behavioral changes? How can we align our entire organization around the Loop?

Change needs to happen on two levels: the organizational level and the individual level. If we try to change the organization but the individuals don't want to change, we're doomed to failure. On the other hand, if the individuals want to change but that change isn't supported by the organization, the change will peter out.

Change at the Organizational Level

Transforming to genuine customer-centricity is a complete philosophical, cultural shift. It takes alignment from the top level of the organization all the way down, and, again, it is not a casual thing. Just as the human body resists "invasion" from foreign particles by attacking them and seeking to restore balance, organizations unconsciously try to eliminate the unfamiliar and restore balance. The bigger and more complex the organization, the harder it is to change. That's why change needs to be *managed* in a comprehensive way.

CHANGE MANAGEMENT

Changing mindsets isn't a one-off thing. Issuing edicts from the head office or writing new policies and procedures are not enough to make organizational change happen and stick. Change must be carefully *managed*—with investment, commitment, and energy—over a sustained period of time. Months for small changes, years for big ones.

Toward that end, it helps to use a change-management model. There are several good models kicking around the business world—such as the Kotter eight-step model, the McKinsey 7S model, and the Lewin model. Ultimately, though, which model we use is less important than the decision to use a model.

At TPG, we use the Prosci ADKAR model.

Awareness of the need for change

Desire to support the change

Knowledge of how to change

Ability to demonstrate skills & behaviors

Reinforcement to make the change stick

Using this model helps companies meet the objective of becoming more customer centric.

- **A: Awareness of the need for change.** Change starts here. This is the stage where we're *thinking* about changing because the Funnel's not working for us: We're not generating enough demand. We're missing sales targets. We've got customer attrition. We're disengaged from the customer. Something needs to give, and we're starting to realize it.

- **D: Desire to support the change.** Based on this awareness, there must be a strong desire on the part of one or more leaders to switch to a customer-centric model, such as the Loop. This desire must be communicated to the whole leadership team, and there must be buy-in at all levels. Too many times I have seen a team getting excited about a change, only to have an executive walk in at the last minute and say, "Yeah, we're not doing that." Alignment from top to bottom is critical.

- **K: Knowledge of how to change.** Now the requisite expertise about *how* to implement the change must be acquired. This can mean hiring consultants (such as TPG), getting key team members trained, and/or distributing literature and other content to everyone. A comprehensive plan for the change must be developed. There must be a deep self-recognition that we're going to have to change a *lot* of things: our marketing processes, sales processes, service processes, what we're measuring with our data collection, some of our core technology.

- **A: Ability to demonstrate skills and behavior.** Next, whether it's through a pilot program, new hires, or skill training, we must be able to show our people exactly *how* we're going to be doing things differently. We need to model what our new behavior is going to look like at all levels of the organization. How does customer-centricity look and feel for *our company specifically*?

- **R: Reinforce to make the change stick.** Finally, we have to cement the change through constant reinforcement in the form of ongoing training, reporting, coaching, reward systems, content distribution, and cultural language and rituals. No matter how much fanfare we employ when rolling out a change, if we don't reinforce it over and over, it's going to fizzle out the way so many change initiatives do. The momentum of the Funnel will pull us back in again.

ADKAR is a handy reminder of all the things that need to happen organizationally in order for change to have a chance.

Change at the Individual Level

In order for organizational change to stick, there needs to be a genuine commitment to transformation at the individual level as well. If the individuals don't change, old habits and mindsets will continue to taint all customer relationships.

Often we hear that people are resistant to change. But actually, most people aren't *entirely* resistant to change. Most people *want* to change for the better. They want to grow. If they can be convinced that a change will be good for them and their families, they will not only be *willing* to change, they will become *ardent advocates* for the change.

> **People want to be *agents* of change. They don't want to be *told* to change.**

The key is this: People want to be *agents* of change. They don't want to be *told* to change. The biggest cause of divorce is one partner trying to change another. People want to own their change. For that reason, buy-in is absolutely essential. People must become excited about the change. They must believe in its value.

But even belief and excitement aren't enough. If they were, then all those New Year's resolutions would stick. The problem is that when we start to attempt transformation, we soon discover that we can't transform everything all at once. There are many small and incremental changes that need to happen. And incremental changes take time. Along the way, we encounter roadblocks and frustrations.

Our resolve is tested. We become discouraged.

Think about the decision to run a marathon. The *decision* is exciting—going out and buying the new running shoes and the books. The training, not so much. When we start to realize how many things must change—diet, sleep, work schedules, family life—and how long and slow the training will actually be, our commitment is tested, and most of us drop off.

Unless we have great training, coaching, and support.

Changing to the Loop is like training for and running a marathon. It's a long, comprehensive journey. If we want our people to embrace it, we have to (1) get them excited so they own the change and (2) support them throughout the process and into the future.

Tying Organizational Change to Individual Change

So organizational change and individual change must be yoked together if the change is really going to stick. In order for this to happen, the organization must recognize the predictable stages individuals go through when dealing with change. Organizations must address these stages of individual change as they accomplish their own change goals.

At TPG, we use this model:

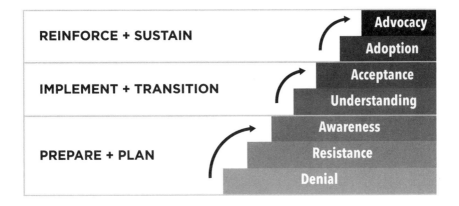

In this model, there are three major stages we go through in organizational change. As we progress through each of these stages, we must address *multiple* stages of individual change that our people are going through.

1. PREPARE AND PLAN

This is the stage at which the company leadership starts to prepare the staff and management for changing to the Loop and to make plans for executing the big change. Education and communication are essential here. As preparation and planning are occurring, the goal must be to progress individuals through these stages of change:

- **Denial**—"I don't have a problem with our Funnel." "I don't have a problem meeting quota." "I don't have a problem generating repeatable revenue."

- **Resistance**—"I don't want to change." "You can't make me." "I've been using the Funnel for decades." "My father used the Funnel, and my grandfather used it. It worked for them."

- **Awareness**—"Okay, maybe there's a better way to do this." "Maybe I can meet my quota more easily this new way." "Maybe I can have happier customers."

2. IMPLEMENT AND TRANSITION

As the company is implementing its plans for change and transitioning to the new model, it must ensure that individuals progress to understanding and acceptance.

- **Understanding**—Team members now learn about the new tools they're going to use, the new ways their work will be measured, and the new ways they're going to engage with the customer. They get ready for the change mentally and emotionally.

- **Acceptance**—Employees realize the Loop is here to stay. They say, "Okay, this is the way I do my job now. I don't want to fight it anymore. I want to learn how to do this right."

3. REINFORCE AND SUSTAIN

Here's where, at the company level, we say, "Okay, we rolled it out. We got everybody on board. Now we need to really drive it home." We recognize that changing to the Loop is not a one and done. We must back it up every day, every week, every month, to reinforce our mission and achieve scale. Meanwhile, we shepherd individuals through the stages of:

- **Adoption**—As with our customers, our employees go through an Adoption phase in which they become comfortable and proficient with the methodology, the systems, the processes, the tools, and the technology the Loop requires.

- **Advocacy**—And finally, once they've adopted the Loop, they see the success they're having with it. They become advocates themselves for this new and better way of engaging with customers.

So those are a few very general ideas about how to tackle major change. The main point is that adopting the Loop requires a deep and sustained commitment to change, on both an organizational and an individual level.

As we move on to the rest of part IV, we'll be looking at some specific strategies and approaches we can use to foster company-wide alignment around the Loop.

But first let's look at one major obstacle we'll need to overcome: the vicious and persistent cold war between sales and marketing.

CHAPTER 15

BROKERING PEACE

S o the only way to align our companies around the Loop is by achieving individual commitment through careful and sustained organizational effort.

Easily said, not so easily done. If organizational change were easy, all companies would be doing it successfully, and all companies would be winners. Clearly all companies are not.

We looked at a couple of models of change management in the last chapter, and these are good basic models, but models aren't enough to change an organization. Models are just words and symbols on paper. Without strong leadership, management, and live stakeholders standing behind the new model 100 percent, it all boils down to talk. We're not really doing it, we're just mouthing platitudes. We hold our meetings, and everyone nods and smiles, then just goes back to doing whatever they were doing before.

Nothing changes.

Look at the sports world for an example of this. Why are some teams so perennially … *awful?* Year after year they dependably fail to achieve. I won't rub salt in the wound by naming some of these teams, but you Jets fans know exactly what I'm talking about.

These teams go through coach after coach after coach, they change their staff, they change their management, they change their players. Their leaders come out and *say* the right things in public, like, "We are 100 percent committed to building a winning franchise," and often they even seem to *do* the right things, at least superficially. They go out and hire a big-name coach, they bring in sports psychologists, they snag a marquee player.

But still they just cannot seem to win. Why? Because they're not really achieving commitment from the top of the organization down to the individual players on the field.

On the other hand, there are organizations like (it pains me greatly to say this) the New England Patriots that are able to field legitimate championship-contending teams year after year after year (at least until the 2020 season, anyway). Operating under the same salary cap as all other teams in the league, the Patriots have put together an incredible twenty-year track record that is unmatched in football.

How? By achieving that magical combination of individual and organizational commitment. They start by hiring players and coaches who have a winning mindset and an understanding of what the organization is trying to achieve. (And when an individual *doesn't* fit their culture, they release him, no matter how "big" he is.) And then they work extremely hard to instill a winning mentality at every level of the organization, which they reinforce hour by hour, day after day, year after year. They make sure everyone knows what the goal is, what their job is, and how their job contributes to the goal.

It's a ton of work, and it requires constant energy, but the payoff is clear.

A book obviously can't teach anyone how to build the equivalent of the New England Patriots, but it can offer tools and strategies that work if we commit to them. In the chapters that follow, we're going to take a closer look at some specific ways we can achieve alignment around our goal—implementing the Loop—throughout our company and within and between individuals.

But before we do that, it's crucial that we understand the number-one place where commitment and alignment typically break down: the nexus between the Sales and Marketing departments. These two entities are perennially in conflict, and unless we broker peace between them, any efforts toward real change will likely stall out.

The Hatfields and the McCoys

In my years in business and marketing, I've worked with thousands of companies, and I can tell you that across all industries, there is perhaps no feud more consistent or pernicious than the one between sales and marketing departments. Both departments are on the same side, but you'd never know it.

Sales departments tend to feel that marketing doesn't understand the pressure of making sales and doesn't understand the customer.

Marketing departments tend to feel that sales is shortsighted, has inadequate systems and processes, and—wait for it—*doesn't understand the customer.*

Often, by the way, the reality is that *neither* department really understands the customer—because they've both been using Funnels, and Funnels aren't *designed* for understanding customers. But even when the Loop is brought into play, sales and marketing departments have built-in conflicts that need to be resolved.

In order to resolve them, we need to understand them. Let's look at some of the main sources of tension in the sales and marketing world ...

HISTORY AND CULTURE

As I noted earlier in the book, only in the last fifteen or twenty years has marketing been asked to be accountable for driving leads, let alone revenue. Sales, however, has been accountable for driving revenue since the beginning of time. So sales has had a much longer time to build a culture around performance. Performance is in the DNA of sales teams.

Marketing was viewed differently for many, many years. It was seen as a cost center. It was given a budget with which to do its "arts and crafts" thing—messaging, product packaging, trade show launches, public relations, communications—but was not asked to drive actual demand.

So Sales tends to feel it understands the ground game far better than marketing does and tends to view marketing as dwelling in a bit of an ivory tower. Marketing thinks sales can't see the forest for the trees it has to go chop down every day.

TIMELINES

Another issue that causes conflict is that sales typically operates under much shorter time frames than marketing does. Sales is perennially under pressure to meet quotas. And if they don't hit their quota, they're out. So sales tends to think small picture first, big picture later. It looks first at the week, then the month, then the quarter, and then the year.

Marketing, conversely, tends to think in longer and more strategic terms. It conducts *campaigns*. It looks first at multiple years, then at this year, then this quarter, then this month.

These divergent timelines create mismatched priorities on a daily basis.

COMPENSATION

The way the two departments are compensated in most organizations also leads to natural tensions. Sales receives commissions based on its bookings. So if they perform, they get paid. If they don't perform, they starve. Survival is the name of their game.

Marketing typically gets paid on a salary basis and operates under management-by-objectives. These objectives are not necessarily tied to bookings and revenue.

UNDERSTANDING OF THE CUSTOMER

Salespeople typically interact with customers quite frequently—on the phone, in person, at trade shows. So people in sales feel they have a much better understanding of what customers want. Because they actually talk to them.

Marketing folks, for their part, tend to believe *they* have a better understanding of customers because they have the data. They look at market research, analysis, demographic statistics, buying patterns. They commission research to get a better understanding of their market. They use focus groups. They send out customer questionnaires and do benchmark surveys.

Though they don't typically spend a lot of time talking to customers directly, marketing people think they have a more sophisticated understanding of how customers *actually* behave and what they *actually* want. After all, the numbers don't lie.

JOB COMPLEXITY

Job complexity is yet another issue. Not to insult sales, but its role is relatively one dimensional: Go out and find prospects. Qualify them. Close them. Done. Not easy, but relatively simple in terms of focus.

For marketing, however, filling the pipeline and generating revenue is just one of the many things they do. As noted earlier, marketing has many customers besides *the* customer. Marketing has to serve the needs of the market analysts; it has to serve product marketing, engineering, sales, R&D, partners, the CEO, the board. Marketing also has to manage technology. In most companies nowadays, marketing manages more technology than IT does. So marketing's job is actually a lot more diverse and complicated than sales'.

To use the football analogy again, a salesperson is like a player whose job is to move the ball down the field. That job has its own unique set of challenges, for sure. But a marketing person is like a coach who has to answer to the front office, the other coaches, the fans, the press, the box office, and the game plan. When a coach calls a given play, he may be taking a host of factors into consideration, from selling more tickets to testing new players' skill sets. It's not *just* about advancing the ball.

GOALS

Sales and marketing often don't even have the same goals. A VP of sales may be measured on how much pipeline and revenue they generate for the quarter. A VP of marketing may be measured on whether or not they get the new website launched. And while the website might be strategically important, the company's stock price probably won't tank because the website didn't launch. But if sales misses its targets, you'd better believe the stock price will suffer.

Those are just a few of the built-in tensions we need to recognize if we want to broker peace between the Hatfields and the McCoys.

Mutual Misunderstanding

As with most long-standing rivalries—liberals vs. conservatives, labor vs. management—a little mutual understanding can go a long way. Both sales and marketing feel the other should walk a mile in their shoes. For sales, it's, "You don't know what it's like being on the firing line every day. Not knowing whether you're going to have a job next month. Having to hunt and kill for your food. You guys have it so easy over there. And by the way, you keep wasting our time by sending us bad leads and content that nobody reads. You can't get us a reference, and you don't seem to know what's happening on the ground."

From marketing's POV, it's, "You guys never follow up on the leads we give you. You never fill out the fields in the database. You never give us feedback on what we're giving you. You never follow up on what we send you. So we feel like we're chasing our tail over here. And by the way, our job is not just to generate demand. We have five million other things to do."

For most companies, this scenario plays out over and over and over again. Sales is on the fifty-yard line in hand-to-hand combat saying, "We need fresh legs in here. Now! Where the hell *are* you guys?" And marketing's response, from way up in the box seats, is, "Trust us, we can see things from here that you can't see. Our game plan is working, you'll see when we get to the third quarter." To which sales responds, "We're not gonna live that long!"

THE CONSEQUENCES

As long as both sides continue looking at the field from only their own vantage points, the feud of mutual misunderstanding will go on. That means there will continue to be missed targets for both marketing and sales, and missed quotas. The two departments will continue to be out of sync on definitions of sales-ready leads and on processes for ensuring speed-to-lead. Folks will continue to generate insufficient pipeline and inconsistent bookings. There will continue to be longer-than-necessary sales cycles, higher churn, and inefficient conversions, leading to lower velocity, poorer close rates, turnover, and loss of morale.

And yet, when the two teams really work *together*, all of these issues diminish substantially or completely disappear. I have seen it over and over. When sales and marketing truly see themselves as one team instead of two groups pulling in different directions, that's when the winning mentality begins. That's when the two groups start to have each other's backs. When the defense has a bad game—to use the football analogy once again—the offense can pick it up enough to score some extra points. Or when the offense can't move the ball, the defense can play tight, keep the score close, and give the offense a chance to win.

If we want to align our company around the Loop, we need some solid methods for building support between departments and individuals. That's the only way we will ever be able to shift departmental agendas, especially in the sales and marketing divisions.

So in the final chapters of this book, we're going to take a look at some practical strategies we can use to foster alignment within our organization, not only between sales and marketing but across all departments.

CHAPTER 16
CLARIFYING ROLES

When tension exists between two parts of an organization—e.g., sales and marketing—there is a tendency for one department to blame the other when things aren't running smoothly and when goals aren't being met.

It is very common under such conditions for a culture of blame to settle in. A blame culture is extremely dangerous in an organization. It creates a toxic work environment in which resentment and finger-pointing reign. When people blame others for problems, they also (perhaps unconsciously) hold those others accountable for providing the solution. Which means they stop accepting accountability and responsibility themselves.

When blame reigns, people become afraid to take bold action for fear of being blamed, so they fly below the radar. They stop taking risks and sharing new ideas. People adopt a narrow and self-protective view of their roles, saying, "That's not in my job description." There's a feeling of anxiety in the air—*Am I going to be the next one whose head gets chopped off?*

It is especially difficult to effect sweeping change—such as adopting the Loop—within a blame-driven environment. Instead of "owning" the change and committing to it, people hold back, waiting for others to take the risks and make the first mistakes. They look for signs that the change is failing and then blame others for the failure.

For that reason, it is best to address tensions between departments early and often. Don't allow tensions to fester into blaming. One of the best things we can do in this regard is to *clarify roles*. Make sure everyone knows exactly what their role is, how it fits into the overall strategy, what the expectations of the role are, and how those expectations will be measured and rewarded. When roles are crystal clear, blaming and anxiety go down, and morale goes up.

Hence the purpose of this chapter.

Improving Clarity from a Structural Standpoint

Before we talk about clarifying individual roles, let's talk for a moment about how we can support greater clarity from an organizational perspective. Many organizations are coming to believe there should be one sales and marketing organization, run by a chief revenue officer, in which sales and marketing are on the same team with shared goals. This organizational change makes sense in many ways—the mere act of fusing the two teams into one can remove some of the rivalry and create a more cooperative dynamic.

Blending sales and marketing may better reflect today's realities. After all, customer behavior has changed radically, as we've been discussing. Customers now control the buying process via the internet. Customers no longer accept cold calls as they once did. The old sales approaches no longer work. And marketing is now much more involved in the selling process. Research suggests that strongly aligning sales and marketing can lead to a 32 percent increase in revenue, a 36 percent increase in customer retention, and 38 percent higher win rates.[7]

But there are some caveats. First it is vital that the person running the combined organization has experience in sales and, preferably, in marketing as well. Blending the two units just won't work if the person in charge has run only marketing and never run sales. No matter how strong their personality is or how good a leader they are, if they've never actually interacted with customers and closed sales—or had to rely on commissions to survive—they won't be able to relate to the sales team. And the sales team *will* call them out for it.

Similarly, if the person in charge has not taken the time to really understand marketing, they'll probably run the department like a sales organization as opposed to a sales and marketing organization. And they will miss the mark. They need to understand how to use the leverage of marketing to drive more revenue, and they also need to understand that marketing's job is not *just* to drive revenue. Marketing has many other jobs to do as well.

Second, putting the teams together in the same unit won't work if *they still have different goals.* Just because they report to the same leader

---

7   Steven MacDonald, "How Sales and Marketing Alignment Increased New Revenue by 34% (Case Study)," SuperOffice, February 2, 2021, https://www.superoffice.com/blog/sales-marketing-alignment/.

doesn't mean they're aiming for the same things. A common example of misaligned sales and marketing goals is a product pricing strategy that is out of whack with the sales compensation strategy. Marketing prices a product with the goal of increasing market share, while the sales team is being incentivized to maximize profit margins. They're playing two different games. No wonder they're at odds.

Goal misalignment is incredibly common. As consultants at TPG, we constantly see companies where, for example, VPs operate fairly autonomously. There might be five or ten VPs all reporting to the CEO. Theoretically they're on the same team—they all report to the same person—but they all have their own budgets, opinions, personnel, resources, and ideas on how they're going to get the job done. And what we find is that the most dysfunctional companies are those where the VPs are all doing their own thing and not working together. Even though they're "on the same team," their goals don't necessarily mesh with those of the other VPs.

So sales and marketing need to be pulling the same levers together. And if they are, then it doesn't matter too much whether they are in the same department or separate ones. We can still have our traditional sales organization and marketing organization, but they need to have shared outcomes, and there needs to be cross-organizational alignment. So if we have a field sales organization, there should be some type of field marketing organization that works with them. If we have a channel sales organization that works with partners and retailers, there should be a partner marketing function, and so on. We need to build multiple bridges between the two groups and create opportunities for them to work together with shared goals.

Guidelines for Clarifying Goals

Once we've structurally established a system of shared goals and shared outcomes—regardless of how the teams are actually organized—we can go about the business of clarifying *individual* roles and objectives for the people on the teams we've now set up.

This starts with establishing the specific path we're going to use for getting closer to the customer. In other words, we design a customized Loop for the customer, and then we begin to execute on it.

As we first go about setting up some of the new Customer Expansion stages, they may be unfamiliar not only to the customer but also to the people within our own company. People may have heard the terms before—onboarding, adoption, value realization, loyalty—but they've never really done anything at an organizational level to address these stages.

So we need to specify roles and responsibilities clearly. The following guidelines can help.

1. **Explain the task.** First the task must be explained to the person responsible for carrying it out. To illustrate this, let's take a fairly simple task (as opposed to a whole *initiative,* such as building an onboarding program, which can be rather complicated). A *task* is a specific step within an initiative. So let's say that as part of onboarding, we decide we need some emails written by one of our marketing writers. We might sit down with her and say, "Laura, as you know, we won the contract with BigFatCorp, and so we want to build a great onboarding program. One of the things we'd like to do as part of that program is create a series of welcome emails for the various touches that are going to happen in the first two months. I loved the emails you did for TechnoNerd, and so

I'd like you to write and design eight emails with that same feeling and aesthetic that we can send out to BigFatCorp."

2. **Explain the reason.** Every task should be explained within the context of the greater purpose it is going to serve. The more people who know about *why* they're doing their task, the more ownership they take. "The reason we're doing this is that we learned that some of our customers have been feeling a bit abandoned after the sale, and we want them to feel valued and welcomed. We also want them to have a better understanding of how our services unfold from day one and the steps that are going to happen in the first two months."

> **The more people who know about *why* they're doing their task, the more ownership they take.**

3. **Check for understanding.** When explaining tasks, remember: communication is a circuit. We send it out, and then it must come back to us to be complete. So first we need to explain the task, then we need to establish that the recipient received and understood it. We can ask, "How do you feel about doing these emails? Do you have any questions? Do you understand what I'm asking you to do? Can you explain it back to me in your own words? Great! Can you give me a little idea about what kind of approach you'll take?"

4. **Provide any necessary instructions.** Next we make sure the task assignee has all the instructions and information they need to complete the task as required. "I'd like you to work with Suzy over in marketing communications first. She can show you the points we need to hit. And please see Chuck in delivery so you can grab some of the tools and templates we

make available to our customers when they sign up."

5. **Give the task a priority designation.** We also need to let the assignee know how urgent/important the task is relative to other responsibilities. "I know you've got a couple of other projects you're working on, Laura, but this is an important priority. I still want you to do that contracting thing as your top priority, but this needs to be your main secondary priority."

6. **Set goals and deadlines.** Finally, we must make all the dates and deliverables clear. "We need this done within the next sixty days. Which means you'll need to submit your first drafts to Jerry in forty-five days so we'll have time to do revisions. Is that reasonable? Can you do that?"

And we do a similar process with all the tasks that need to be performed at each stage.

Engage the Right People at the Right Time

A major aspect of the Loop is that the customer owns their own journey—but everyone in our company still plays a role in *engaging* with the customer at various points in that journey. It can be clarifying to map this out visually. Here's a sample:

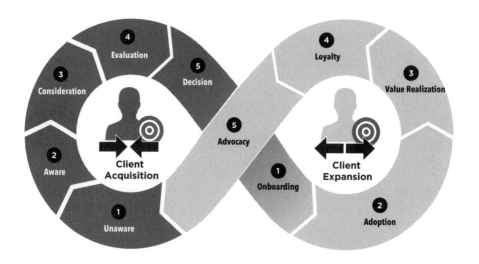

1	Marketing	Sales	Services
Unaware			

1	Marketing	Sales	Services
Onboarding			

2	Marketing	Sales	Services
Aware			

2	Marketing	Sales	Services
Adoption			

3	Marketing	Sales	Services
Consideration			

3	Marketing	Sales	Services
Value Real.			

4	Marketing	Sales	Services
Evaluation			

4	Marketing	Sales	Services
Loyalty			

5	Marketing	Sales	Services
Decision			

5	Marketing	Sales	Services
Advocacy			

The graphic shows the ten "standard" stages of the Loop, with a visual indication of which departments (here we look only at marketing, sales, and service) are involved, and to what degree, at each stage of the Loop.

In stage 3 of the Client Acquisition side (evaluation), for example, both marketing and sales are heavily involved, while service is minimally involved. However, in stage 2 of the Client Expansion side (value realization), marketing and sales are minimally involved, while the main burden of engagement falls on service. A customized version of this graphic can be useful in visualizing, planning, and scheduling resources.

RACI Role Mapping

Another excellent management tool for clarifying roles within a company is a RACI grid that shows which team or individual is responsible (R), accountable (A), consulted (C), and informed (I) for various jobs at various stages.

A RACI map can be used to further clarify and specify roles within the Loop.

		Inside Sales	Outside Sales Rep	Director of Sales	Sales Manager	Customer Service	Marketing	Finance	Implementation
Onboarding	Program Design and Management								
	Develop Content								
	Facilitate Communication								
	Develop KPIs								
	Expectation and Goal Setting								
Adoption	Blueprint								
	Plan								
	Measure								
	Segment								
	Engage								
Value Realization	Plan Capabilities								
	Value Management								
	Operational Model and Governance								
	Resource Management								
	Customer Management								
	Decision Support								
Loyalty	Program Design and Management								
	Identify Loyalists								
	Develop Relationships								
	Facilitate Communication								
	Develop Content								
Advocacy	Identify Advocates								
	Develop Relationships								
	Facilitate Communication								
	Develop Content								

I: Informed

C: Consulted

A: Accountable

R: Responsible

INDEX:

In this example, we break down the Loop stages into specific processes, and we show the people and teams that might be assigned to these processes in order to operationalize the Loop. In onboarding, for instance, someone needs to design and manage the onboarding program. Who's accountable? Who's responsible? Who needs to be consulted, and who only needs to be informed? Someone needs to develop content. Someone needs to drive the communication with our customers, and so on. We go across and down the grid, putting R, A, C, or I in each box.

We can also use this RACI role-mapping process to plan in more general terms around the main business functions we're trying to accomplish by using the Loop.

		Inside Sales	Outside Sales Rep	Director of Sales	Sales Manager	Customer Service	Marketing	Finance	Implementation
Relationship Management	Account Discovery								
	Key Influence Mapping								
	Strategic Account Planning								
Opportunity Management	Lead Generation								
	Recognize Need								
	Search For Information								
	Evaluate Alternatives								
	Resolve Concerns								
	Deal Approval								
	Implement Solution								
Delivery and Support	Train Customer								
	Support Customer								
	Exception Management								
	Determine Segment Movement								

INDEX: R: Responsible A: Accountable C: Consulted I: Informed

The reasons we're using the Loop are that we want to (1) manage relationships, (2) create and manage opportunities to drive revenue, and (3) deliver and support our products and services. So within these major functions, we ask, *What are some of the main processes that need to occur?* The grid here shows some examples.

We might want to add some processes or take some out; this is just an illustration. Every company's grid will be a little different. But you get the idea. We start by asking, *At our company, what are the major things we do to build relationships, manage opportunities, and deliver and support our products and services?* And then we ask, *Who is responsible, accountable, consulted, and informed in each of these areas?* We don't need to boil the ocean here; we can use as much or as little detail in the grid as is useful in our particular situation.

Clarifying roles makes everyone more effective and removes hidden tensions. In the following chapter, we'll look at the next key step in achieving company-wide alignment around the Loop: incentivizing change.

INCENTIVIZING CHANGE

A dopting the Loop—making the decision to become more customer centric—represents a huge change for a company. And in most cases, it's a "voluntary" change, which means it isn't being *forced* on the company by immediate circumstances, such as a COVID-19 outbreak or a corporate merger. Forced changes often carry their own brand of incentive—people *have* to adapt if they want to survive and have a job.

In the case of changes that are done in a more proactive way, though, such as shifting to the Loop, change really needs to be *reinforced* in a consistent way. Otherwise it won't stick.

There are two forms of reinforcement we can use, negative and positive. Many companies and teams, even in today's "enlightened era," tend to rely on negative reinforcement. Employees are yelled at, pressured, threatened with job or pay loss, or punished in various ways to "motivate" them to change. Fear is the operating factor here. Fear *can* be partially effective on a short-term basis, but a culture of fear burns people out and has diminishing returns.

Positive reinforcement has been shown to be far more effective in the long run (and the short run as well). Praise, encouragement, reward, respect—these are the things that really incentivize people and bring out the best in them. And so if we want change to happen—e.g., shifting to the Loop—we must create an effective incentive structure of some kind.

Coming up with the right balance of incentives is an art form unto itself. Let's dig into the topic a bit so we can think about it more clearly.

External and Internal Incentives

What kind of incentives are available to us?

Generally speaking, incentives can either be delivered internally (by our organization) or exerted upon us by external factors. An example of an external factor is a huge and unexpected turn of events that an industry faces—think about the airlines or the restaurant business dealing with the COVID-19 crisis. Or perhaps a brand-new technology or a huge new competitor arrives on the scene. In the wake of such external changes, we must adapt fast. Otherwise we're not in business anymore. When a hurricane is coming, you don't need an artificial incentive to motivate you to fortify your house and boat. You just hunker down and do it.

External factors aren't always negative. They can be positive too.

CHAPTER 17: INCENTIVIZING CHANGE

An opportunity to bid for a huge new project or a sudden opening of a new market can be exciting and motivating enough to push everyone into high gear. For a while.

Internal incentives are created artificially by the company to drive new or sustained behaviors. Internal incentives can be dictated by external factors. An external demand for new products, for instance, or an increase in customer complaints can motivate a company to change. Internal incentives can be tied to such external incentives. For example, bonuses might be awarded to customer service staff for putting a new customer reporting system in place to improve customer satisfaction numbers.

When it comes to devising internal incentives, it's important to remember that no two employees are wired the same. People are motivated for different reasons. Some people are heavily motivated by compensation, others by recognition, others by career growth, etc. What works for one employee will not work for everyone. But whatever incentives we come up with should tie back to our objectives for implementing the changes in the first place. They should also correspond with our methods for measuring success.

> **Whatever incentives we come up with should tie back to our objectives for implementing the changes in the first place.**

FINANCIAL AND NONFINANCIAL INCENTIVES

Ultimately, incentives break down into financial and nonfinancial categories. Some people are motivated almost exclusively by financial incentives; others hardly at all. So in most cases, we should employ a mixture of both. And they should be tailored, as much as possible, to the types of personalities we're dealing with in various parts of the company.

CHAPTER 17: INCENTIVIZING CHANGE

An opportunity to bid for a huge new project or a sudden opening of a new market can be exciting and motivating enough to push everyone into high gear. For a while.

Internal incentives are created artificially by the company to drive new or sustained behaviors. Internal incentives can be dictated by external factors. An external demand for new products, for instance, or an increase in customer complaints can motivate a company to change. Internal incentives can be tied to such external incentives. For example, bonuses might be awarded to customer service staff for putting a new customer reporting system in place to improve customer satisfaction numbers.

When it comes to devising internal incentives, it's important to remember that no two employees are wired the same. People are motivated for different reasons. Some people are heavily motivated by compensation, others by recognition, others by career growth, etc. What works for one employee will not work for everyone. But whatever incentives we come up with should tie back to our objectives for implementing the changes in the first place. They should also correspond with our methods for measuring success.

> **Whatever incentives we come up with should tie back to our objectives for implementing the changes in the first place.**

FINANCIAL AND NONFINANCIAL INCENTIVES

Ultimately, incentives break down into financial and nonfinancial categories. Some people are motivated almost exclusively by financial incentives; others hardly at all. So in most cases, we should employ a mixture of both. And they should be tailored, as much as possible, to the types of personalities we're dealing with in various parts of the company.

Financial incentives, naturally, are part of most organizations' systems of reward and recognition. Employees can be rewarded with salaries, bonuses, commissions, equity in the company, retirement benefits, and financial perks such as health insurance, car allowances, educational benefits, and more. Financial incentives are important; how many people would turn up to work every day if they weren't paid? However, they are only part of the picture.

Nonfinancial incentives can cover a wide range of options. For example:

- **Reputation enhancement.** For many people, the opportunity to shine among their peers is hugely rewarding.

- **Career progression.** Promotions and other methods of advancing employees' careers are essential motivators. Many of these, of course, have a financial aspect as well.

- **Sense of accomplishment.** The satisfaction that comes from working with a great team and bringing a challenging project across the finish line is irreplaceable. Giving teams the tools and autonomy to design projects and see them through to fruition can be extremely motivating.

- **Creative challenge.** For some, the opportunity and freedom to solve a problem in a new way or create something that has never existed before is all the motivation they need.

- **Client feedback.** Positive feedback from customers/clients can be quite reinforcing. For example, the service team earns four and a half smiley faces from customers this year when they earned only three and a half smiley faces last year. It's highly gratifying to know, "Hey, we did something about that. We worked on something together, and our customers are happy."

- **Training and development.** Training opportunities are highly valued. One thing I did recently for my executive team, for example, was to pay for an executive coach people can work with on their own time or during company time. This was a way of saying, "We're investing in your career, and we care about your development."

- **Mentoring.** The opportunity to receive one-on-one mentoring from someone whose knowledge and experience we treasure can be worth its weight in gold. Serving an "apprenticeship" under a "master" is often a highly sought opportunity.

- **Recognition and awards.** An employee-of-the-month certificate or a special award given at an annual meeting tells people their service is noticed and appreciated.

- **Events and trips.** Sending people to professional conferences and training events or inviting them to off-site executive retreats can be greatly incentivizing. Free vacations or weekend getaways can also be given in recognition of achievement.

- **Praise.** Simple acts of praise—a "thank you" or a "job well done"—cost us nothing but mean a great deal to people. Lack of appreciation is one of the main reasons people leave jobs.

- **Increased importance to the company.** People yearn to contribute and create value in their organizations. When we give team members more responsibility, we're saying, "We trust you with this important task or role."

- **Improved facilities.** Providing high-quality recreational and dining facilities, for example, is a great way to incentivize people to work at a company—also, on-site gyms, day care facilities, and aesthetically pleasing offices. One of Google's early draws as an employer was the fun and creative work space it provided for team members.

- **Work flexibility.** Flex schedules or the opportunity to work from home can be massively incentivizing for many.

- **Gamification.** "Gamifying" some tasks and goals by making them inherently fun and rewarding can be a great incentivizing tool. Contests for excelling in specific areas is another way to gamify the work environment.

It's good to mix "generic" incentives—the kinds of things that make people want to work for our company in general—with incentives that are tied to specific goals, measures, and accomplishments. Emphasis on the latter.

Incentivizing Sustainable Change

Change, as I've said, is a marathon, not a sprint—especially a change as comprehensive as switching to the Loop. So if we really want to drive change, that change must be *sustainable*. It's easy to get someone to do something in the short term by offering them a carrot and stick, but if we want someone to be part of a marathon with us, we need to think long term.

To incentivize change on a sustainable basis is a four-step process:

1. Create habits

2. Break habits

3. Provide up-front incentives

4. Remove barriers

1. CREATE HABITS

The secret to creating any kind of sustainable change is to build new habits. There is a whole art and science to habit-building, which we can't get into in a single chapter. (Two great books on the topic are *The Power of Habit* by Charles Duhigg and *Atomic Habits* by James Clear.)

The first thing we want to do is make a list of the new habits we want to create in order to encourage people to become more customer centric. What are the specific behaviors we want to see happening differently than before?

To make this list, we should consult with key people in every department and then narrow the list down to three to five habits we really want to focus on with each team (trying to change too many habits at once doesn't work). These might include things like: *asking* the customer what they want versus just *assuming* what they want, calling the customer to see how they're doing, or taking steps to determine whether or not the customer is getting value.

And then we look for ways to measure or track these habits and find ways to incentivize them, repeatedly and consistently, over the long term.

2. BREAK HABITS

Hand in hand with the building of new habits comes the breaking of old ones that no longer serve us. In the old Funnel mindset, for example, habitual questions we asked were, "When's the deal going to close?" or "How much have we sold today?" We don't necessarily want to stop asking such questions, but we must remind ourselves that such questions serve only *our* internal forecasting, not the client. We must modify our habit to include questions like: "What needs have I uncovered in the last month for my clients?" "What challenges have my clients been saying we can't solve?" "What are some deals we lost to our competitors, and what did those guys do differently to earn the client's trust and business?"

As leaders and managers, we must monitor the resurfacing of old habits and provide timely, positive, real-time feedback to team members on how to do things "the new way."

3. PROVIDE UP-FRONT INCENTIVES

Getting our team to start changing their behavior is no easy task. So we need to create excitement up front in the form of early incentives. "Hey, we're going to have an Onboarding contest. Which of our customers can have the best Onboarding experience?" or "Let's see how many advocates we can create in the next three months. Whichever product line gets the most wins a trip to Hawaii." Get people excited about doing the things they weren't doing before.

4. REMOVE BARRIERS

And then, of course, we need to take inventory of all the things that are getting in the way of becoming fully customer centric. Is there a stakeholder or executive who isn't really buying in? Is there an antiquated technology or process that's gumming things up? Is there some way we've organized our structure that needs to change? Are there toxic elements in our culture?

Sustainable change is all about finding the right sets of behaviors, incentivizing them, and clarifying roles so that we're getting the outcomes we want on a consistent basis.

A Few Things to Keep in Mind

When designing incentive programs, here are a few points to remember:

INCENTIVIZE AT ALL LEVELS

Incentives must appeal to multiple levels within the organization. If we incentivize only the executives and fail to get the managers online or fail to engage the employees, we won't get very far. Conversely, we can drive all the behavior we want at the field level, but if the leaders are undercutting the change because they don't believe in it, then nothing's going to happen either. A good balance of incentives across the organization is essential.

DO GROUP AND INDIVIDUAL INCENTIVES

It's wise to have a mix of group and individual incentives. Group incentives—where the whole team receives some kind of reward for achievement—are terrific because they enhance a sense of team. Everyone encourages one another, which lifts performance to new levels, and people also hold one another accountable if they're not pulling their weight. But individuals should also be incentivized in ways that work for them personally. In sports, for example, the whole team is incentivized to win the championship, but players are also rewarded for hitting individual milestones.

LET PEOPLE IN ON THE BIG PICTURE

When implementing the Loop, it's important to let everyone know *why* we're doing it in business terms they can relate to. Saying "We want to be customer centric" is too simplistic and vague. Let's say we're in a subscription company, and we have a high churn rate—that means we're leaking money because we're losing too many customers. Maybe the reason we're putting the Loop in place is to try to improve customer retention. So make that clear. Make sure everyone understands the problem the Loop is being implemented to solve and also understands how solving the problem will help them personally and individually.

WATCH OUT FOR TRAPS

Incentives are meant to support a business in the achievement of its goals. However, they can also have unintended consequences. For example, merit-based incentives that reward *some* employees but not others may disincentivize those who aren't rewarded. Nonfinancial rewards, such as invitations to training events or workshops, may be seen by some employees as a reason wages aren't higher. ("Why don't they spend that money on our salaries instead of on *that* [bleep]?") There's also the danger that creating an incentive-based culture may cause people to adopt an attitude whereby they apply themselves only if an incentive is offered. Finally, a mismanaged incentive scheme can encourage cheating and unethical behavior (think the Wells Fargo account fraud scandal) and discourage teamwork.

CHANGE INCENTIVES PERIODICALLY

Even with the best incentive plans, it's important to change them up every now and then because we never want an incentive to feel like an entitlement. For example, when an annual bonus gets paid at the end of the year no matter what, people come to expect it. In their mind, it is part of their salary package, so why change their behavior? A bonus should reward behavior and results that go above and beyond the norm.

Well-thought-out incentives are an integral aspect of making change stick. Now let's look at another integral aspect: effective planning.

CHAPTER 18

MAKING PLANS

aking a change in the fundamental way we do business—i.e., implementing the Loop—requires careful planning. No matter how good an idea is, no matter how much sense it makes for everyone, we can't just wave a magic wand and expect the change to embed itself in the company. We must be strategic and consistent about it. We must plan effectively for how we're going to get people on board and for how the specific changes are going to occur.

That means good communication planning and good project planning.

Making a Communications Plan

Whenever we're planning to make a change across an organization, the first thing we need to think about is communication. We need to communicate *why* the change is needed, *what* the change will entail, *how* the change will happen, *when* the change will happen, and *what* the expected benefits and challenges of the change will be, among other things.

Mainly, we need to make sure everybody in the company is aligned with the change and can understand it through the lens of their own role.

One of the best ways we can accomplish these things is through a great communications plan. Most companies are well aware of the need for good communications, but far fewer are aware of the need for a good communications *plan*.

How to Write an Effective Communication Plan

After years of helping clients create communications plans at TPG, we've found there are several key steps that can help ensure it's done right.

WRITE A CHARTER STATEMENT

The best way to start designing a communication plan is to come up with a charter statement to kick things off. We ask ourselves, *What is the purpose of the communication plan? What are we really trying to accomplish here?*

In the case of switching to the Loop versus the Funnel, using the Loop is not really our *true* goal, is it? Our true goal is probably something much broader and more important—such as, "We want to fundamentally change the way we engage with our customers, from the initial sales efforts all the way through delivery, and build a more relationship-based approach." The Loop is just a model we're going to use to get there, not an end in itself. Making a clear and impactful charter statement about our business aim is the first step toward clarifying our own goals and getting everyone in the company to understand them.

DO A STAKEHOLDER ANALYSIS, AND PLAN THE MESSAGING

With any type of major change, getting everybody on board is critically important. We need buy-in from sales, marketing, and marketing leadership. We need finance, the C-suite, and products and services aboard. Why? Because this kind of change impacts the entire company. If we don't have the right stakeholders supporting it and putting their weight behind it, it's doomed to fail. So we need to figure out who the key stakeholders are and how we're going to message each of those stakeholders differently.

AUDIT COMMUNICATION MATERIALS

In modern business, communication occurs in myriad ways. We can email. We can host internal portals. We can use collaboration software like Slack or Microsoft Teams. We can have town hall–style meetings, in person or on Zoom. We can use company newsletters, Facebook pages, Google Docs, hard copy delivered in person, and so on.

The fact is, we're probably already using a dozen communication methods across our existing business initiatives. We don't need to start from scratch when communicating internally. So we want to perform a communications audit in which we list all our current communication capabilities and how we can use them to communicate effectively with all our stakeholders. We can then figure out where the gaps are and how to close them.

SET SMART GOALS FOR COMMUNICATIONS PLAN

Next we set SMART goals for the communications plan. That means, again, that the goals are Specific, Measurable, Actionable, Realistic, and Time-Bound. What goals are we setting in our implementation of the Loop? Perhaps we plan to implement an onboarding program by the end of the first quarter. That's specific. So it should go in our communication plan. "Becoming a customer-centric organization," on the other hand, is not a SMART goal. It's a vision, but it's not specific and actionable.

IDENTIFY THE AUDIENCE

Once we've set our goals, we need to figure out who the audience is for each communication we're going to send out around each goal. Again, this goes beyond sales and marketing; many people in many departments may be impacted by putting in the Loop. IT, for example, might be an audience to address because we're going to need some new systems in place to create our loyalty program. Customer service might be an audience to address because we're planning to change service requests into something broader and more strategic. Finance might be an audience because we're planning to change our incentive and compensation plans to reward more customer-centric behavior, and so on.

DRAFT THE PLAN

Based on all of this, we sit down and actually outline and draft the plan. We decide things like: *Here's what we want to say first, second, third, and fourth as we roll this plan out. Let's do message A weekly, message B biweekly, and message C monthly.* And so on.

PLAN AND DEVELOP ASSETS

Now we decide what assets we need for each part of the plan. Customized emails? Infographics? Is there going to be a video? Are there going to be trainings? Video training or live training? Do we need workbooks for the training? All of these assets need to be written, designed, and produced on a schedule that meshes with the overall plan.

DETERMINE THE CHANNELS

We've already done an audit of our communications methods. Now we want to get specific: Which channels are we going to use to deliver each part of the communication plan? Here's where we make the specific decisions. We will probably want to use multiple channels. Email? The web? An online collaboration platform? An internal company app? Our intranet?

ASSIGN THE WHO

We also need to be crystal clear about who will be delivering each message. Is it the CMO or the chief revenue officer who'll be sending out Message A each week, or will it vary each week depending upon the topic? And if it is coming from multiple people, how do we make sure that the tonality, the language, and the messaging is consistent? Someone needs to be in charge of that aspect too. Who will it be?

APPOINT PEER ADVOCATES

Just as we need to develop advocates for our products and services, we also need *internal* advocates who can help us carry our Loop messaging to their peers. This is a bit like building a political ground game; we need to get a grassroots movement going within the company. This starts by identifying a couple of employee advocates in each team or department who are well respected and will throw themselves behind this effort. We must obtain their full buy-in and incentivize them somehow. And then we just turn them loose to spread the message in their own way. "Hey, Bob, I've got a buddy over at United. They put the Loop in last year, and boy, they're really starting to generate some revenue now."

ESTIMATE A TIMELINE FOR HOW LONG EACH STEP SHOULD TAKE

Creating a timeline is foundational to a good communications plan. *What* and *when* to communicate. The *what* includes communicating milestones, best practices, anecdotal successes, and KPIs. The *when* represents the cadence of the communications. Pacing is an important consideration.

It's important to build in some sprints to go along with the marathon. Not everything has to wait a year before being implemented. We want some early wins, so look for things that can happen in the first week or two. Small things can overlap with bigger things.

> **We want some early wins, so look for things that can happen in the first week or two. Small things can overlap with bigger things.**

We also need to prioritize those steps that will have the biggest impact to the business at the lowest cost. And we want to make sure the change occurs in digestible chunks and we don't try to do everything at once.

MEASURE THE RESULTS OF THE PLAN

Finally, we need to measure the impact of the plan. We come up with some internal KPIs—indicators that the communication is working. Or not. For example, we might look at quota achievement, employee attrition, content engagement, ramp-up time for new sales and marketing people, whatever helps us measure how successful we're being at driving the change. We also use subjective measures. What are people saying? What's the energy level and the mood of our people now? What's the level of conflict—has it increased or decreased?

Change in and of itself can be a lot for a company to manage. But the amount of change is never as much as the amount of communication required to see it through. And the more people we have in a company, the more energy we need to spend communicating. A thorough communication plan is essential for driving the change and getting people on board.

Project Plan

Good project planning is essential too. As I've said many times (perhaps ad nauseam), implementing the Loop is no simple task. It can involve a lot of areas—technology, content, process changes, documentation, training, personnel, organizational changes, budgeting, and more. So we're going to have multiple work streams with multiple tasks, multiple critical paths, multiple assignments, etc.

All this needs to go into a project plan.

There are countless ways to manage a project. Again, it's not so important which approach we use, it's just important that we *have* a systematic approach. Here are the planning phases we use at TPG, but these are not absolute by any means. Think of the following more as a checklist of steps you'll probably want to include in any project plan you create. The steps can apply to the overall process of implementing the Loop or to individual projects within the overall process.

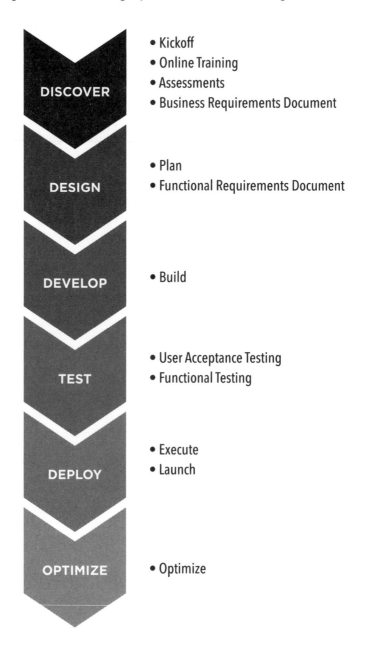

- Kickoff
- Online Training
- Assessments
- Business Requirements Document

- Plan
- Functional Requirements Document

- Build

- User Acceptance Testing
- Functional Testing

- Execute
- Launch

- Optimize

DISCOVER

When kicking off any project, there is always an element of self-discovery and assessing. We assess our systems and technology capabilities, our content, our marketing, our current skills, our personnel, our processes. We look at our data quality and storage, our reporting and analytics, our ability to generate insights, our culture, our predisposition toward change and innovation. We look at our governance—how might it slow us down?

We also do a risk analysis of some kind—where are our areas of highest risk in making this change?—and assess where our greatest obstacles and challenges will lie.

Essentially, this is the time for getting our arms around the scope of the project. The plan will look very different depending upon how big its scope is. Are we in a start-up company with a small CRM and a small marketing platform? Are we in a global enterprise with twenty instances of CRM, seventeen instances of marketing, multiple business units, and multiple budgets? The bigger the company and scope, the more complex the plan, obviously.

This is the stage where we write our business requirements doc too. What are the high-level business needs and aspirations we are trying to accomplish by making this change? How do we think this change will help us get there?

DESIGN

Armed with our assessments and our business requirements, we set forth to design the project plan. What's the functional set of requirements we need in order to pull it off—the technology, the processes, and the people? We capture this in a functional requirements doc.

In the design phase, we also get people to sign off on the plan and its scope. The danger in this phase is that we create a thorough project plan and set a realistic scope—and then people keep changing it. Small changes here and there can be okay, but big changes are a big deal. So our aim here is to lock a design down as early as possible—something that meets the critical needs for a first-phase rollout. We can always add more scope for phase two, but it's better to accomplish something concrete within a reasonable time frame than to lose momentum because the plan keeps getting bigger and less manageable.

DEVELOP

Once we have agreement and sign off on all the functional and technical specs, we build it. We configure our systems, and we design our nitty-gritty processes. We build our documentation, our content, our training programs, and our communications.

TEST

From here, we go into testing. We go back to the functional and business and technical requirements documents, and we test against them. We pressure test the systems, conduct some user-acceptance assessments, test the customer experience, do some dry runs.

DEPLOY

Once we've made any needed adjustments based on our testing, we launch. We execute on the project plan. We set our wheels in motion.

OPTIMIZE

Once we've done our rollout, then over time we optimize it and tweak it—essentially forever. Perhaps, for example, when we designed our original Loop, we wanted to have four steps on the Client Acquisition side and six steps on the Client Expansion side. But then we come to realize we need seven steps in Client Expansion. Or maybe we were happy with our onboarding program at first, but after doing it for a year, we decide to tweak some of the communication steps.

So the project is a living, breathing thing. We do our concrete steps—define the work, validate it, build it, test it, launch it—and then we keep coming back to it in a circle and reevaluating. What are the new requirements now that our business goals or our outcomes have changed? Where can we optimize and make the system better?

Again, project plans are as varied and complex as the companies that implement them, but these steps provide a basic framework that can be adapted as needed.

Now let's take a look at one final aspect of aligning our companies around customer-centricity: training.

CHAPTER 19

TRAINING FOR THE LOOP

T he final major element that needs to be considered when making a sea change like adopting the Loop is culture. No big change can take place in business unless the business culture aligns with it.

Culture is the human software of a company. It is the unseen set of rules, habits, and behaviors that dictate everything that happens in a company, from the way employees talk to each other to the way clients are handled to the way the office furniture is arranged. Culture is the pulse of an organization, the "feel" you get the moment you walk in the door. Do people love their work? Do they treat each other with respect? Do clients feel like they're a welcome part of the "family"?

Is there positive energy in the air? A dynamic sense of organization?

Or is there sullenness and disorder? Do clients/customers feel like they're intruding on something more important when they walk in? Are processes more important than people?

Developing a customer-centric culture is not a casual thing. It requires a fresh mindset from everyone from the top leadership to the frontline staff. And culture doesn't change on its own; it must be trained into people and then reinforced again and again and again.

Elements of Training

Just as with a communications plan or a project plan, there isn't one set way to train for the Loop, but there are some common elements and principles that can help us tailor a training plan for our company's specific needs. So whether we plan to train in person or through an on-demand platform, whether we intend to train through videos or by bringing in outside speakers—or by a unique combination of methods—here are some principles and ideas to keep in mind about training.

DEFINE THE CUSTOMER-CENTRIC CULTURE

Square one is to establish a clear and well-defined picture of what we're aiming for as a culture—much as we did when writing a charter for our communications plan. What do we want our culture to be?

It's relatively easy to make small and specific customer-centric changes in a company. We can train someone on how to use our marketing systems better. We can teach a salesperson a new script. We can teach a marketing person how to develop a new piece of content. But unless we have an *overall* cultural matrix in mind, we might get small behaviors to change, but we'll miss the bigger picture.

The specific changes will have no cultural soil in which to grow.

So it's crucial to define what we want the future state of culture to look like. What does it mean, *for our company specifically*, to have a customer-centric culture? How does such a culture feel? How does it behave?

When defining a culture, ask probing questions: What are some ways we can connect every aspect of the company back to the customer? What does a customer-centric office layout look like? How does a customer-centric phone call sound? How does a customer-centric business meeting unfold? What does customer-centric decision-making sound like? How might a customer-centric incentive program work?

Coming up with specific answers to these and similar questions will flesh out vague ideas about customer-centricity and give us a clear idea of what customer-centricity looks like *for us*.

COMMUNICATE THE CULTURE

Even more important than any formal culture training we do for staff is the steady stream of communication and messaging we send out in support of the cultural change.

Imagine you ran a company that was historically very engineering oriented. At your big annual training event, you tell everyone, "Okay, guys, this year our vision is to become more customer centric and less product centric," and you do a few team-building and roleplaying exercises. Everyone cheers and goes away feeling awesome. And then … nothing. You don't send out any other communication or materials or whatever. The people who were at that training are going to forget the message pretty quickly. Old habits will resume. Old mindsets will remain.

So we have to make sure communication and materials go out

every week to reinforce the future vision we want. After a while, employees will begin to realize, "I'm getting material about this constantly. Guess they were serious about this stuff, I should probably pay attention."

People learn in different ways—some learn visually, some aurally, some experientially—so our messaging needs to go out in many different forms and media. It can include printed materials, emails, spoken announcements, signs and posters, videos, interactive exercises, or physical changes to the office space. Customer-centricity (however we define it specifically for our business) should become a focus of every business meeting and every piece of training going forward. It should become part of the language that is spoken and written on a daily basis.

HIRE TO THE CUSTOMER-CENTRIC CULTURE

If we're committed to customer-centricity, we need to evaluate our hiring practices too. In the past, when we were a product-oriented culture, we probably looked for the standard types of qualities when hiring—people who met our corporate values, showed up on time, had relevant experience and education—and we probably asked the standard questions. "Can you tell me about your experience doing *blah, blah, blah?*" But we probably didn't look for customer-oriented personalities and characteristics.

If we want to build a customer-centric culture, it starts with the screening and interviewing process. Instead of asking the typical "Where do you see yourself in five years?" questions, we must ask questions that test and measure for customer orientation. "Give me an example of how you dealt with a challenging customer or client." "What are some things you put in place at your last job to be more customer centric?" "What are some things you would do here over the first ninety days to help ensure that you're addressing our customer needs?"

If our company is large, we might even consider using a group format for our first round of interviews. Explain the culture to the collective group of candidates first and allow anyone who doesn't wish to be part of it to leave. Then, mixing candidates for all positions together, do some group exercises and games, observing the way candidates relate to others. Look for empathy, listening skills, problem-solving ability, cooperation, and "people skills" in general.

Not only do we want to hire customer-centric people, but we also want to communicate to new hires, from the literal first minute they arrive, that customer-centricity is the company's number-one value. We establish this during the hiring process.

TRAIN *EVERYONE* TO THE CULTURE

Training people to the culture is essential, but here's a vital point: that means training *everyone*. One thing we've noticed at TPG is that companies that miss the mark on the Loop are often those whose leaders feel they're above training. Their attitude is, "I already know this stuff, I don't need training. Training is for frontline people, not for top-tier leadership."

This attitude sends the message that the leaders don't think the training or content is important. So even though employees may attend the training because they're required to, they don't pay nearly as much attention as they would if their managers and leaders were sitting in the training right next to them, asking questions, taking notes.

Even the CEO—especially the CEO—should go through the training and should actively participate. This communicates the message "Nothing is more important than this training. We're all in this together. We all have something to learn. I do too."

MODEL THE BEHAVIOR

On a related note, it is also vital that all employees—but especially leadership and management—*model* the behavior that is essential to customer-centric culture as we define it. We all must, as Gandhi famously said, "*Be* the change we want to see in the world."

How well does it work when we tell our kids they should eat better but we're ordering fast-food cheeseburgers every day? Or when we tell our spouse they should exercise more but we never pry ourselves off the couch? Same thing when we ask employees to be more customer centric but then turn around and tell our sales team, "We need to get our numbers up by Friday!" and tell our marketing team, "Let's get more campaigns out the door—we need more leads!"

That's not modeling the behavior; that's not *being* the change. That's saying, *Do as I say, not as I do.*

One of the great challenges of leadership is that we must *embody* the qualities and behaviors we're asking others to exhibit. So before even attempting a change like switching to a customer-centric business model, we need to ask ourselves if we are willing to *be* that change ourselves. If not, then we shouldn't even attempt the change; it will only fail.

Of course, being human, we will make mistakes. We will slip into the old habits. But when this happens, we can correct ourselves and make it a learning experience for everyone.

OPERATIONALIZE CUSTOMER EMPATHY

Operationalizing customer empathy is another important element of changing culture. Customer empathy means putting ourselves in the shoes of the customer and asking, *What does the customer need? What do they feel? What would I want right now if I were in the customer's position?*

We can *tell* our employees to be more empathetic, but unless we give them specific behavioral ways to practice empathy, it won't happen.

One simple piece of advice I give people all the time is, "When your clients call, pick up the phone because they're probably not calling to say hi." It's so easy these days to let a call go to voice mail and then sent a text or an email reply later, but picking up the phone and talking to someone in real time is the best way to tell them they're important to you.

What if we're sitting down to dinner with our family when a call comes? We can still greet the client warmly, find out why they're calling, and say something like, "I'm really sorry your systems went down. That must be incredibly stressful to you, what with your campaign launching next week. I'll tell you what. I'm sitting down with my family right now, but I want you to know this is going to be my top priority first thing in the morning. And I will call you about it before nine o'clock tomorrow morning to work out a solution. You have my word."

In this way, we can honor our family time while still making the effort to listen and hear the client's concerns. Developing habits like this help us put empathy into action. Some other empathy-empowering habits include: letting the client speak first, letting the client speak fully without interrupting, reframing a client's concerns in our own words, and offering empathetic feedback ("I can see why you're feeling upset, I would be too") before leaping to solutions.

EMPOWER EVERYONE TO BE A CUSTOMER-CENTRIC LEADER

One of the best ways to operationalize customer empathy is to empower all of our staff to be service leaders. In other words, give them the green light to resolve customer issues on the spot. We've all had the frustrating experiences of sitting in a restaurant and we just need a fork or a napkin, so we ask a server, and they say, "This isn't my station, I'll see if I can find your waiter." And then we wait ten minutes for a fork while our food is getting cold. Or we're at a ball game and we drop our hot dog, and the vendor tells us they'll have to radio a manager to resolve the situation. It would be so much better if the guy just handed us a new hot dog and said, "Don't worry about it."

Empowerment means training staff to handle customer/client issues and giving them the latitude to provide solutions on the spot, in their own way. Of course, the solution must be appropriate to the problem. If the hot dog vendor not only replaced our hot dog but also gave us a hundred dollars' worth of free merchandise, that response would be disproportionate to our issue. So guidelines and limits also need to be provided.

What does employee empowerment look like in a B2B setting? Well, if a client felt they weren't getting the right support, the employee might say, "Okay, I'm going to extend your contract by thirty days," or "I'm going to personally take care of this issue myself. I'll call you by five o'clock today, and here's my personal phone number."

One of the best ways to empower all employees is by sharing the information we already have. I've talked about this before. Give everyone the ability to pull up the customer/client's file and see the client's history instead of having them transfer the call to another department and then another and then another. "I see this is the third time you've called in. You shouldn't have to spend your valuable time calling us. I'm going to personally address this problem and find out what's going on. When is the best time to call you back?"

FACILITATE DIRECT INTERACTIONS WITH CUSTOMER/CLIENT

Along these same lines, we should also facilitate direct interactions between our employees and customers. Instead of setting up layers of interactive voice response systems and chat robots and FAQ lists, make it easy for staff to get on the phone or get on video and talk person-to-person with clients and customers.

RECOGNIZE GREAT EMPLOYEE PERFORMANCE, AND TIE COMPENSATION TO THE CUSTOMER

When employees do something great—i.e., perform an exemplary act of client care—it's crucial to recognize it and make a big deal of it. This not only rewards the exceptional employee but also tells the other employees, "This is the kind of client treatment we value."

Years ago when I owned a Subway sandwich shop, there was an incident in one of the company's Midwest stores that became famous within the company and earned some press outside the company. A robber came into the store and demanded all the money from the cash register. An employee of the store recognized that the man was hungry and stressed out, and offered him a free meatball sub. The robber was so grateful, he left without robbing the place. The employee became a company hero.

> **Being customer centric is not necessarily the same thing as being more efficient, and it's important for staff to know we value the former more.**

There are plenty of opportunities—at weekly meetings, at annual events, in company newsletters—to share stories of great customer-centric behavior. Whenever possible, we should also tie *compensation* (raises, bonuses, etc.) to the customer-oriented behaviors we want to see. Compensation drives behavior. Being customer centric is not necessarily the same thing as being more efficient, and it's important for staff to know we value the former more.

IMPLEMENT THE RIGHT TECHNOLOGY

Of course, implementing the right technology is critically important too. The bigger the company, the better the tools we need to have in place to automate functions that can help us have better customer interactions. The right technology helps us scale our culture, relate to customers more easily, and solve customer problems more effectively. The wrong technology has a dehumanizing effect and puts a wall between us and the customer. It tells the customer our system efficiency is more important than they are.

So these are always the dual questions we must ask: "What technology could we implement that would make this experience more pleasant and seamless for the customer?" and "How does this piece of technology we're considering buying improve the customer experience?" If we can't answer the latter question, we shouldn't buy the tech.

CELEBRATE SUCCESS

Last but not least it's important to celebrate our wins together.

When we become more customer centric, we drive up renewal rates, bring in more revenue, earn higher customer satisfaction ratings, get more referrals, become more profitable, gain market share, and generate more advocates. We reduce complaints, attrition, product returns, and interdepartmental friction. There are many, many wins a company scores when it gets customer-centricity right. And all those wins should be celebrated, with a clear tieback to the customer-oriented behavior that produced the win.

Again, training for the Loop will happen differently at every company, but if we hit all these points, we have a great shot at making customer-centric culture a foundational aspect of our company.

COMING FULL CIRCLE—CLOSING THE LOOP

O ur journey began with a question: *Why don't our companies love us?* And it wasn't a vain or academic question. It was a question rooted in a profound and enduring dilemma: without the respect of our peers, our marketing departments don't have the authority or the credibility to execute on their missions—the very missions that drove us to choose careers in marketing.

Many of us end up isolated and frustrated as a result of this dilemma. If you spot a person in a suit at the end of a bar, staring into a drink, looking a bit lost, there's a decent chance it's a disillusioned marketing person.

Early on in the book we established *why* our companies don't love us: they don't love us because they don't see us as a revenue center. They *expect* us to drive revenue, sure, but they still *see* us as a cost center—because of our "arts and crafts department" history.

Solving that problem, it turns out, isn't easy. It requires a new mindset. And changing mindsets is tough, we've discovered.

In order to transform ourselves from a cost center into a revenue center, we've had to take a hard look at the narcissistic, formulaic way we interact with our customers. Our customers don't love us because we don't love them. Our customers want a relationship, not a transaction. We're used to treating customers transactionally because we've been relying on the Funnel, a sales and marketing model that reflects the assembly-line mindset of the era in which it was invented—an era where sellers controlled the marketplace, and the sales process followed a predictable, linear pipeline. Leads in one end, revenue out the other.

But that model doesn't work anymore because customers now have almost total control of the purchasing process. So we've had to throw out the Funnel and conceive of a new model for customer engagement—one that is organic, adaptable, and authentic. One that puts the customer/client in the center.

And we've had to learn how to *implement* that new model—not only in our own departments but across our entire organizations. It's a lot of work.

But that work *is* worthwhile. Because it helps us create long-lasting, rewarding *relationships* with our customers. And once customers see that we're committed to our relationship with them—that we actually stick around after close of deal—they won't just make purchases anymore. They'll continue to interact with us after the deal is done, adopting our products and services, developing loyalty, and even advocating for our brand. And when their needs change and they need new products and services, they'll come back to us naturally and automatically.

As these types of thing start happening, we're suddenly able to draw a direct line from the marketing department to new revenue. And once our department starts demonstrably bringing in revenue, we can generate the authority and the credibility we need in order to launch bold campaigns, deliver high returns, and ensure job security across our departments.

Not a Push-Button Solution

But of course I don't want to create the impression that the process of adopting the Loop is mechanical, linear, and entirely predictable. It isn't. If you look back at part IV—this last part of the book where we talked about building alignment with sales and other departments—you'll see that the process by which we win organizational credibility through implementing the Loop isn't one of cause and effect. One thing doesn't happen *after* the other.

Rather, things happen simultaneously. In order to implement the Loop model, we have to develop alignment with sales and other departments. The very mission of adopting the Loop requires winning a certain amount of buy-in from our peers up front. So we're not starting at zero credibility and building to a hundred. The nature of loops is that they have no beginning and no end. But they do bring new rewards and new possibilities each time they cycle around.

We businesspeople tend to want quick fixes. We buy new technology, we hire new execs, we change our packaging or marketing—

we pull business levers, and we expect business outcomes. But our expectations will be out of whack with reality if we expect the Loop to be a push-button solution. To change a company to being customer centric is a long-range, comprehensive undertaking. It's not something that can be accomplished in thirty to sixty days.

That's not to say we can't get short-term wins along the way. We can. We can start to see some real and immediate impact within a couple of months, but we won't have the whole thing done in a couple of months. No way. Not even close. However, the sooner we start the journey, the sooner we'll get there. And the journey can still be rewarding and fulfilling along the way.

Wrapping Up

Everything starts with a thought. The greatest inventions, the greatest social movements, the greatest achievements in human history all began as a thought in someone's mind. And that's the purpose of this book. To get you thinking new thoughts: New thoughts about how to reach out to clients and engage them where *they* need engaging. New thoughts about the relationship between sales and marketing and how the two can work together to be more customer centric. New thoughts about the very purpose and philosophy of your business. Does your company exist for you or for your customer? Give that some real thought. And be honest.

> **Does your company exist for you or for your customer? Give that some real thought. And be honest.**

After reading this book, you might well come to the conclusion, "You know what, Jeff? I like your ideas, but the Funnel is working just fine for me, thank you very much." If that's the case, I'm happy for you. Seriously.

It's not my intention to shove these ideas down anyone's throat.

But if reading this book has piqued your interest in a new way of doing business, I do want to assure you: this stuff works. It isn't just pie-in-the-sky aspiration. We've used it at our own company—after all, *we're* a client-oriented business too—and we've seen it produce amazing results for our clients over and over.

If you think you might be interested in exploring the idea of implementing some or all of these ideas at your company, the TPG team would be delighted to talk with you. As I mentioned at the start of the book, we have been doing this work for thirteen years. We've helped over 1,500 clients around the world digitally transform their businesses, build better customer experiences, implement better Loops, and adopt processes that drive scalable revenue in today's digital world.

If you want to find out more about the work we do, give us a call.

But whether you choose to work with us or not, I hope your "customer experience" with this book has been a good one. I'd love to hear your thoughts. You know where to reach me.

See you in the Loop.

ABOUT THE AUTHOR

Jeff Pedowitz is the president and CEO of The Pedowitz Group (TPG), a consultancy that helps clients change the way they get revenue. TPG helps companies create and execute new business models for driving repeatable, predictable, and scalable revenue in a digital world.

Jeff has over twenty-five years of experience leading successful B2C and B2B organizations. Widely recognized as an industry expert and thought leader, he frequently writes and speaks on a variety of topics related to Revenue Marketing™, demand generation, marketing operations, and marketing technology. Jeff hosts a weekly podcast, *CMO Insights*, where he interviews sales and marketing executives on the topics of business transformation, digital transformation, and the customer experience. He lives in Alpharetta, Georgia, with his wife and business partner, Cherie; his three children Alex, Zach, and Ashley; and their three dogs—Safari, Magic, and Maya—and a cat, Odie.

ACKNOWLEDGMENTS

t really does take a village. This book could not have been possible without the amazing support system I had. First, Andy Wolfendon, thank you for working with me every week for three months. Your calm and reaffirming presence, along with your amazing gift for the written word and attention to detail were the driving force behind completing this work. I can't imagine working with anyone better. Aaron Fischer, thank you for a great book plan and for putting together the construct of the story. David Taylor, thank you for your graphic design and creative genius. Kristin Hackler, thank you for managing all of the writing. Kristin Goodale— project manager supreme!—thank you for running such a tight ship and getting us over the line three months early! Nate Best, editorial manager, your keen insights and observations really brought the book together. James Wilcox, thank you for putting together a great marketing plan and I am so excited to see your ideas come to life. Caroline Nuttall, our account manager, thank you for introducing us to the Forbes Family and for being such a great partner through all of this. We wouldn't be here without you.

To my team: Majda Anwar, our fearless director of marketing, thank you for working so hard to make this book a success. Your creative and strategic input has been invaluable. To my partner, Dr. Debbie Qaqish, thank you for reviewing this book, not once but twice, while you were busy writing a book of your own. I am forever grateful for your friendship and insights. To Laura Yeste, our logistics manager and Queen of Making Sure Everything Gets Done, thank you for keeping everyone and everything on track and on schedule. To my partners, Scott Benedetti and Gary Flicker, thank you for all of your support and encouragement and for investing in this project. To my leadership team, I am so grateful I get to work with you every day. Thank you for all that you do: Evan Whitenight, Rebecca Barkan, Kevin Joyce, Lori Haberman, Caitlin Poliska, and Marina Slabyak.

To my family—Cherie, Alex, Zach, and Ashley—thank you for all of your encouragement and support. I couldn't do it without you. To our TPG team, thank you for all that you do. Thank you for living our values of integrity, results, innovation, service, and wellness. Your relentless pursuit of excellence. Your obsession with getting results. Your commitment to your craft and to our clients. I am so eternally grateful.

And finally, to our clients. Thank you for putting your trust and confidence in us every day. You are the living embodiment of the Loop. We are energized by our partnership and committed to your success.